C

and

Whiting & Birch
Publishing

Other titles in the Groupwork Monographs Series

Groupwork Relationships (ISBN 9781861771056))

Structured Groupwork (9781861771063)

Groupwork with Older Adults (9781861771087)

Groupwork with Children and Families (9781861771094)

Groupwork and Social Action (9781861771100)

Groupwork Research (9781861771070)

Groupwork and Women (9781861771124)

Groupwork Monographs
Series Editor: Oded Manor

Groupwork and Mental Health

Edited by
Oded Manor

With an introduction by
Gabrielle Richards

W&B
MMX

ISBN 9781861771117

Printed in England and the United States by Lightning Source

Groupwork and Mental Health

Contents

Preface

Each of the books in this series is an anthology of groupwork papers dedicated to one theme within the area of groupwork practice. The books can be used in a number of ways:

- *Practitioners* may draw on the ideas when considering their planned and current practice.
- *Students* may explore this pool of knowledge when expanding their understanding of groupwork.
- *Teachers and trainers* of groupwork may choose papers that direct their students to certain features of this method.
- *Researchers* may look for references that are still relevant to their particular area of study.

All will be invited to sample a pool of knowledge that has accumulated within the pages of the Journal *Groupwork* over almost two decades.

The series Groupwork Monographs is published by Whiting and Birch whose support of the Journal over the years has been vital. Ideas that had been initially raised in the editorial board of the journal led to these publications. We felt it would be good to offer readers a carefully selected collection of previously published papers. Papers that have withstood the test of time and can still meet current needs were sought. Indeed, re-publishing these papers is in itself a kind of message. We wanted to highlight the value of exciting groupwork knowledge and its relevance to current practice. In doing so, we wanted to encourage practitioners, students, teachers and researchers to enrich their practice through familiarity with this reservoir.

As the Series Editor, I reviewed all the papers published in *Groupwork* since its inception in 1988. This combing through previous publications was a very moving experience. Faces that I had known so well over so many years re-appeared and struggles in which I had participated came back to the surface. I felt privileged identifying appropriate papers and grouping these according to their themes. Sadly, some themes included too few papers to make a viable book. Of the viable themes some were well outside my direct experience and I asked various members of the editorial board of Groupwork to take responsibility for developing these into books.

Where my experiences as a practitioner, supervisor, researcher, teacher and editor in groupwork seemed fitting I undertook to form the actual books and invite specialists to write an introduction to each. I asked these specialists to comment on the contents of each paper, on the connections among the papers, and on the relevance of all to current practice and policies.

I think you will find these introductions very helpful – I certainly learnt something from reading each. I hope you will discover in each book something to go back to, so you can more easily go forward in developing, sustaining and enriching groupwork practice.

Oded Manor
Series Editor of Groupwork Monographs
London 2010

Note from the Publisher

Approach to production
This volume comprises material published in *Groupwork* over several years. No textual amendments have been made, apart from the silent correction of a few spelling errors (that is, the *words* are exactly as originally published), and all but two of the chapters in this volume have been produced directly from the computer files of the original setting (the other two were produced from scans of the originals). Original heading levels and the like have also been retained. 'Keywords' have been added to earlier articles where not originally provided.

The *Groupwork* house style has been modified slightly over the years, and there will therefore be some inconsistency of referencing style between the chapters in this book.

Over the years, there have been changes in the typeface used for *Groupwork*, and, all chapters have been recast in a single face (for those interested, Berkeley Oldstyle Book 10/12pt).

Citation
Authors citing material in this volume should recognise the original date and journal provenance in accordance with the house style of the publication for which they are writing, either by citing material as the original periodical article, or, if citing this volume, by clearly indicating the original date of publication of the material both in text references and in the bibliography. Assuming the house style of your publisher is based on Harvard, the reference list entry will look something like:

Home, A (1996) Enhancing research usefulness with adapted focus groups. *Groupwork*, 9, 2, 128-138 (Reprinted 2009, in O. Manor (Ed.) *Groupwork Research*, pp.82-92. London: Whiting & Birch)

The citation in the text will look something like: Home (1996/2009).

Author contact details
Authors' details are as at the date of publication. In case of difficulty in contacting any author refer to the publishers (enquiries@whitingbirch.net).

Introduction

Garbielle Richards

It was a pleasure to have been asked to write the introduction to this book. As an occupational therapist who has been using groupwork as a cornerstone of my practice over many years, this book has been able to provide further insights into a whole range of possibilities. For many it will be a confirmatory experience, where the articles presented will support and consolidate their practice. For others the examples and available evidence will act as stimuli for change and an impetus to do things differently. The book may well also wet people's appetite to read more about groups, want to develop their skills and appreciate the real examples of the competences and interventions needed for groupwork.

No doubt, this book will be welcomed by students and practitioners alike from any profession working in mental health. It will potentially encourage further research, as some of the articles suggest.

The design of this book is a form of innovation. It is a collection of articles published in the journal Groupwork focussing on mental health. You will find here a range of groupwork activities, analyses and expertise that have been built up in this field, illustrating a range of groups used in mental health as seen through different lenses.

People function in groups whether they have a mental health problem or not. They are, for example, part of everyday groups - work teams, religious, political, family or social groups. Whether people feel socially included contributes to their emotional well being, which is enhanced through feeling part of a group and of a wider society. Conversely, being and feeling part of a group or community can help to combat some of the exclusion individuals experience when they struggle with mental distress. This is so because their illness can isolate and exclude those individuals. Participation in groups of their choice can assist them in recovering lost roles, reassessing current roles or developing new ones.

Historically, much of the treatment for people with mental health problems has been carried out in groups. Groupwork practice still continues today, despite a sea change to a focus on individual one-to-one care. Many people who work in mental health have had some degree of exposure to, or training in groupwork. Such experiences might have been in a community group on an inpatient ward, an activity based creative group in an occupational therapy department or a staff support group. Many of these situations may help; from learning on the job what a group is, to understanding group concepts, processes and the complexities of group dynamics, through good supervision and formal training.

But how often do we take stock and reassess what we are doing in our groupwork practice? How often do we review the evidence? Update our thinking? Consider it in the context of current policy drivers? Reflect on what others have done and recommended? This book has provided the opportunity for just these things.

*

The book is divided into sections focussing on groupwork relating to different care groups. With its eclectic mix of both research articles and descriptive pieces, it could be considered to have a 'something for everyone' approach.

Chapter 1 provides a good overview of groupwork in community settings, outlining many of the difficulties and dilemmas practitioners experience in successfully running groups. These range from the time pressures of case load management to the fact that many feel they have not received specialist training in Groupwork techniques.

Chapters 2, 3 and 4 drill down and provide some interesting insights into groupwork with people who struggle with psychotic difficulties, each with a distinct focus.

Chapter 2 makes good use of case study examples to illustrate the roles groups can play in working with negative, positive and disorganisation symptoms. Creating supportive group environments are created for people experiencing their first psychotic episode, encouraging patients' involvement in research and working with cultural diversity. The chapter provides a strong argument for the use of special groups for those suffering the early onset of schizophrenia.

Chapter 3 is an article reviewing the outcomes of empirical studies on multi-family interventions. It appraises a whole range of interventions relating to working with families and makes recommendations for future work and research.

Conversely, *Chapter 4* is a simple and practical article describing the 'how' of setting up a group. It provides interesting and anecdotal examples as a guide.

Chapters 5 and 6 are articles about groupwork for people with non-psychotic difficulties. Both are quite different in their focus.

Chapter 5 details a pilot study on the effectiveness of groupwork for stress and anxiety. Many practitioners will find this article useful as it provides evidence that groupwork can be effective for anxiety and stress management in community settings. I'm sure that for many readers this chapter will resonate with the National Institute for Clinical Excellence (NICE) guidance and the proliferation of services aimed at increasing access to psychological therapies.

Chapter 6, with the exotic title 'Cycling over Everest: Groupwork with depressed women' provides a fascinating, in-depth analysis of psychoanalytic theories from a feminist perspective in relation to one typical group session.

Chapter 7 describes the nature of the therapeutic community at the Henderson Hospital with an emphasis on working with people with personality disorders.

While chapters 2 to 7 deal with specific psychiatric conditions, *Chapter 8* presents an overall inclusive framework and recommendations for assessing if groupwork is fit for purpose and relevant for community mental health practice.

Finally, *Chapter 9* goes beyond the groups that are run by professionals, turning its attention to the option of self-help. The author describes a research project which reviewed the programme called Grow (part of a self help movement for mental health patients in Australia) and discusses its strengths as well as weaknesses along with recommendations for improving its work.

*

Having briefly presented the chapters in the book it is worth stressing how this book relates to current mental health practice.

First, I would point out to the range of evidence of the impact of groupwork. This range may well contribute towards building the *evidence base* so urgently sought for current practice.

Second, would be the relevance of the various chapters to *Continuing Professional Development* in mental health. As already pointed out, practitioners reach groupwork from many starting points. The current chapters may be one of these launch pads, or may serve to extend knowledge they have already gained.

Third, it may be helpful to remind ourselves of the rapidly changing policy context in which we operate. The proliferation of activity and emphasis on supporting individuals' *recovery journey* is important. Recovery-focussed practice is about seeing people beyond their diagnosis and mental health problems. It is about supporting them as they develop social roles and relationships through paying attention to their abilities, aspirations and interests based on attitude that foster hope and opportunity. In many ways this book highlights examples of how groupwork can continue to play its part in achieving these goals. Indeed, the chapters in this book spring from a groupwork tradition that has stressed for many decades the priority of recovery issues. The groupwork represented here has been a vehicle through which individuals can develop self awareness, enrich their sense of identify, receive support, learn, practice and develop skills that promote their recovery and social participation.

Furthermore, and that may be a fourth point: in the forms of groupwork represented here such an emphasis on recovery is promoted not only by the workers but very much so by each group member towards all the others. The current emphasis on *users involvement is a long established principle of this type of groupwork, and so – the practice examples provided may strengthen the hand of practitioners committed to uses involvement too.*

This book has provided a number of examples and offered insights related to a wide range of areas directly relevant to achieving all four goals.

In summary, this collection of articles has presented a robust case for groupwork. It highlights the range and variety of the potential benefits of groupwork with regard to diversity of client groups and settings. Through the use of previously published articles, it brings together a whole spectrum of insights offered through anecdotal descriptions, case study examples and empirical research. This is a good book for any practitioner working in mental health who wants to touch base with groupwork and reaffirm the use of groups as part of people's recovery journey.

Gabrielle Richards
Professional Head of Occupational Therapy and Lead for Social InclusionSouth London & Maudsley NHS Foundation Trust/Kings Health Partners
Fellow of the College of Occupational Therapists

Using groupwork in community mental health: Practitioners' views

Ben Papps, Oded Manor and Jerome Carson

The current study sought to explore the views of NHS mental health professionals on the use of groupwork in mental health teams. Practitioner views were sought concerning the possible quality of life goals that could be pursued through groupwork, the relevant methods for delivering groupwork and what helped and what hindered groupwork practice. These questions were put to mental health practitioners (N=155) in the South London and Maudsley National Health Service Trust. Their replies suggested that using groupwork to promote positive self-concept was the goal with which they agreed most strongly. Facilitating spontaneous interaction among clients in the group was the method that gained strongest overall support. Believing in the relevance and effectiveness of groupwork was the aspect that appeared to help practitioners most, while difficulties in fitting groupwork into their existing caseload most clearly hindered practice. Most practitioners (63.2%) had never received specialised groupwork training, while 87.5% said they wanted to receive such training. These preliminary findings may be helpful in planning the future provision and evaluation of groupwork interventions within National Health Service mental health settings.

Key words: *quality of life; groupwork models; obstacles to practice*

Background

Groupwork, defined within the context of mental health service provision to service users within the National Health Service (NHS), can be broadly defined as a method of working in mental health settings adopted by professionally trained practitioners when working with a number of clients at one time, who come together to receive services. Simultaneous face to face interaction is actively promoted and groups work towards agreed quality of life goals.

A recent draft proposal on Training Organisation for the Personal Social Services (TOPPS, March 2002) entitled 'The National Occupational Standards for Social Work' included a range of aims designed to capture the increasing importance of group-orientated practice in multi-disciplinary settings. The standards aimed to capture 'the holistic approach of the social worker in their work with individuals, families, groups and communities' The document outlined 5 'key roles' for social work practice in multi-disciplinary settings. These roles included the need to 'contribute to developing and coordinating support networks' by supporting 'people to develop and work purposefully in groups'. The report highlighted the need for mental health professionals to 'identify opportunities to form and support groups. Help groups to achieve planned outcomes for their members and evaluate the appropriateness of their work'.

Groupwork has a long history as a professional form of intervention in mental health in the UK. As a body of practice knowledge, groupwork can be said to be highly developed (MacKenzie, 1997; Manor, 2000a). However, little is known about the extent of actual use of groupwork in UK mental health services. Less is known about the views and practices and, moreover, the skills and competencies of practitioners who do currently offer groupwork orientated services within the NHS. Over the past 20 years there has been an increase in the number of published studies employing groupwork orientated interventions with populations usually served by mental health services. Such populations include for example, survivors of childhood sexual abuse (Watson et al., 1996), HIV positive drug abusers (Pugh, 1995), cancer patients (Daste, 1990), and homeless mentally ill individuals (Martin & Nayowith, 1988). The use of groupwork can be an effective mechanism for providing a wide range of interventions. This may be due to the potential cost-saving implications for the NHS. The medium of provision provides the potential for an increase in the client to practitioner ratio, thereby reducing the costs associated with practitioners' time. This may be particularly relevant for the provision of psycho-educational interventions (e.g. Onyett, 2003). It is also possible that the use of the groupwork model of provision may have additional benefits for the client, over and above those provided in the traditional 'one practitioner, one client' model. For example, appropriately facilitated groupwork may provide environments in which to test newly learnt skills and/ or may provide the potential for the development of robust social support networks within the group. Such interpersonal processes, including the failure to obtain and maintain supportive social relationships have been implicated in the maintenance of mental health problems (e.g. Gotlib & Hammen, 1992).

In principle, the range of services that could be delivered appropriately using groupwork as a medium, is broad. Furthermore, the range of mental health professionals who could conceivably modify or adapt their practice to use groupwork is wide. These include clinical psychologists, psychotherapists, psychiatrists, occupational therapists, mental health nurses and social workers. Currently, it would appear that the use of this 'medium of provision' within NHS mental health services is largely (although not entirely, e.g. Platzer et al., 2000) confined to therapy-based services for various mental health problems (e.g. group 'psychotherapies') and services which aim to teach or rehabilitate skills (e.g. social skills, occupational skills). It is clear that the successful implementation and maintenance of groupwork interventions depend on a variety of group orientated as well as contextual factors (e.g. Doel & Sawdon, 2001; Cowburn, 2000), and the evaluation of such factors is an important aspect of current groupwork research. If successfully implemented, in principle, the use of groupwork could be extended to a wider range of services within the NHS and, additionally, groupwork practice may benefit from a range of theory driven approaches to group functioning.

Less is known about the views, practices, skills and competencies of practitioners who do currently offer 'groupwork' orientated services within the NHS. In order for research on the effectiveness of groupwork practice to be advanced, it is useful to gain an understanding of both the current extent to which groupwork is used within NHS mental health services and the views of those mental health professionals who do and those who do not offer groupwork. For example, how do practitioners think groupwork helps or perhaps hinders their clients' road to recovery? What methods of groupwork delivery are preferred? What service-orientated obstacles, if any, tend to be experienced by those who do not offer groupwork? And what sense is there of the availability and necessity of any training for working with service users in group formats? These questions were addressed in the current exploratory study under a series of broad areas:

- Possible *outcomes* of groupwork when identified as quality of life goals
- Relevant *methods* of groupwork
- What *helps* and what *hinders* groupwork practice
- Is training available, taken up, or felt to be necessary?

Quality of life goals as planned outcomes in groupwork

Research into the quality of life of mental health clients is prolific (Priebe et al. 1999). Yet, quality of life itself has remained relatively ill-defined. This is mainly because the meaning assigned to quality of life depends on the aspirations of those whose quality of life is being described: what is viewed as quality in one culture may not be so highly regarded in another.

The humanistic view is that quality of life increases as each person strives to actualise his or her potential for a richer and more meaningful life (Oliver, 1999, p.85). These aspirations can be broken down into various goals.

The Lancashire Quality of Life Profile (Oliver et al, 1996) can be seen as a list of such goals. The Profile emerged out of research into subjective as well as objective indicators of wellbeing. The Profile incorporated dealing with symptoms (the so-called positive symptoms) as well as increasing clients' ability to get on with their daily life (so-called negative symptoms) (Oliver et al, op cit, pp. 29-47). These authors acknowledge that while there is a tendency to regard the concept of quality of life as a 'rag-bag', many of the underlying concepts are well researched (if not always clearly defined). The most useful definition is 'one which does not exclude any necessary dimensions arbitrarily or precipitously' (Oliver et al, op cit, p. 47).

The major components of the Lancashire Quality of Life Profile (Oliver et al. 1996, pp.251-270) were adapted in the current study as a method of quantifying the effect of groupwork practice. Added to these was 'removing underlying causes of symptoms'. We included this item in order to account for a possible psychodynamic interest within our particular sample. The major dimensions surveyed were the following:

- Increasing clients' *work and education* opportunities
- Enhancing clients' involvement in their own *religious* concerns
- Improving clients' *financial* situation
- Improving clients' *living conditions*
- Helping clients with *legal* matters
- Improving clients' *family* relations
- Expanding clients' *social* relations
- Promoting clients' *health*
- Enhancing clients' positive *self-image*
- Alleviating burden on clients' *carers*
- Helping clients *cope with symptoms*
- Removing underlying *causes* of clients' symptoms

These quality of life goals were seen as potentially dependent variables that could be affected by groupwork orientated mental health interventions. Clients and service users could rate their own 'quality of life' in relation to each of these goals before a service was offered, after an episode of care had ended and at follow up. While quality of life goals may be relevant to any mental health intervention, the focus here was on offering groupwork.

Groupwork methods

Groupwork practice is not of one mould. Many groupwork approaches have been developed – some articulated as models and methods, others remaining sets of guiding principles. Conceptually, a case can be made for different outcomes to be pursued by emphasising different group experiences (Manor, 2000b). The current exploratory study sought to discover which groupwork approaches were preferred by various mental health practitioners.

Practitioners were offered a range of simplified descriptions of well-documented groupwork approaches. They were then asked to indicate the relevance of each approach to their practice. A series of major groupwork approaches were selected – those which have stood the test of time and were likely to be familiar to trained groupworkers. These were the choices that were offered to practitioners:

Cognitive approaches

Followers of these approaches concentrate on group members' largely un-stated beliefs about the right ways of responding to stressful situations. They then systematically help the members alter their views and thereby the ways they respond to such challenges (e.g. Free, 1999).

Behaviour modification

This is a model that focuses on systematically encouraging and reinforcing enabling behaviours on the one hand, and on the other – not reinforcing disabling ones (e.g. Rose, 1977; Rose, 1980; Trower et al. 1978)

Cognitive behavioural approaches

This approach combines the modification of clients' behaviour with changing their thoughts and beliefs. Principles and methods developed in cognitive methods and behaviour modification methods are combined – sometimes into detailed manuals that instruct the practitioner how to conduct each session (e.g. Brown, 1998; Scott and Stradling, 1998).

Mutual aid

Promoting a great deal of cohesion inside the group, practitioners of this persuasion take active steps to encourage group members to help one another outside the confines of the group in their everyday lives. The aim here is to form new networks of informal support among group members and those they know in their neighbourhood (e.g. Gitterman and Shulman, 1994; Shulman, 1999, pp.302-318)

Mediating model

This approach aims to help clients to deal with other professionals in meeting their medical, financial and/or practical needs. The worker positions herself between the group and various external bodies and facilitates a dialogue between the members as a collective and those bodies – be they the sponsoring agency, the courts, or the medical establishment (e.g. Schwartz, 1976; Shulman, 1999, pp.588-592).

Empowerment model

This approach aims to mobilise clients to form pressure groups that lobby organisations in pursuit of clients' rights. Collective social action is the prime goal of this approach. By first articulating a social view of their need, members are then encouraged to take over and lobby organisations for resources they consider lacking (e.g. Mullender and Ward, 1991).

Humanistic approaches

These approaches facilitate spontaneous interaction among clients in the group. Authenticity is the most cherished goal of this approach. Group members are actively encouraged to be honest and spontaneous with one another, as this quality is considered the key to actualising their potential for developing and sustaining relationships (e.g. Brandler and Roman, 1991; Rogers, 1971; Yalom, 1995).

Psychodynamic approaches

The aims of psychodynamic approaches include attempts to elicit clients' unconscious preoccupations and interpret these. 'Making the unconscious conscious' is the hallmark of this approach. Individual and group themes are spontaneously elicited and members are enabled to gain insight into their underlying dynamics (e.g. Ashbach and Schermer 1987; Foulks, 1975; Schermer and Pines, 1999; Whitaker and Lieberman, 1964).

Enactment methods

These methods involve the staging of 'make believe' episodes during which clients enact their own conflict situations. Pretending that a past situation (as in psychodrama) or a present one (as in role-playing) is actually happening in the room, members are directed to enact these in vivo and explore alternative ways of responding to these situations in the future (e.g. Blatner, 1973; Moreno, 1964; Shaw et al. 1980).

Activities based programmes (e.g. Phillips, 2001) and the use of the creative therapies (e.g. Darnley-Smith and Patey, 2003; Meekums, 2002; Waller and Gilroy, 1992) were not included in the approaches to groupwork. While these approaches are widely used in mental health we did not include them here.

Organisational concerns

Community Mental Health Teams have been studied extensively (of special interest here are: Payne, 2000; Onyett, 2003). In spite of this, the particular organisational concerns that arise when practitioners try to offer groupwork have not been included. Indeed, these concerns may explain the relative neglect of groupwork in current practice.

In one-to-one work, intervention with each individual can be organised according to the circumstances of that person alone. The time, the place, the frequency and the duration of contact can be negotiated individually with each service user. However, offering groupwork requires coordinating, in advance, all these aspects so that all members come to the same place at the same time. In addition, the working alliance (Manor, 2000c) in groupwork is more complex too. The working alliance is not only between the worker and the client, this alliance is also among group members. Particular skills are needed to foster and cultivate this more complex relationship (Manor, 2000b, 97-117). This being the case, no specific knowledge seems to be available about the organisational concerns that influence the use of groupwork in community mental health.

The current study aimed to investigate what mental health practitioners thought helped them practice groupwork and what they considered to have hindered their involvement. We did not have a fully articulated framework to draw on when asking such questions so we could only cite clinical and practice experience. Therefore, quite pragmatically - twelve issues that were known to influence practitioner involvement in groupwork were collated. These are listed below:

* Whether groupwork would meet clients' needs;
* The effectiveness of groupwork;
* Any negative effect on clients;
* The amount of work involved in setting up a new group;
* Fitting groupwork into existing caseloads;
* Groupwork being offered by other team members;
* Practitioner's knowledge of groupwork;
* Team members' interest in groupwork;
* Rate of clients not turning up to the group or dropping out;
* Skills of engaging many clients simultaneously;
* Incorporating groupwork within the demands of the Care Programme Approach.

Training requirements

Another question was whether practitioners should receive specialised training in groupwork. Training in group psychotherapy is offered by well recognised bodies such as the Institute of Group Analysis. When it comes to training practitioners in other groupwork methods established courses are difficult to find.

The Department of Health (DoH 1997), Directory of Community Mental Health Training includes about 300 courses. Yet, only six of these mention groupwork training (pp.24, 40, 51, 79, 83, 84). The Department of Health also recognised the ability to work with groups as a requirement for all British social workers. Again, to what extent social workers and others are actually educated and trained to work with groups is unknown.

Purpose of the study

The purpose of the current study was to begin to explore the views of mental health practitioners as regards groupwork practice in a large inner-city NHS mental health trust. We sought the views via the survey of a broad range of mental health professionals who both did and did not offer groupwork in relation to four broad domains.

The first aspect was the views of mental health professionals regarding the viable goals of groupwork. The second aspect of the questionnaire sought their views regarding the applicability of the major approaches to groupwork to the clients served by their teams. The third aspect related to obstacles faced by mental health practitioners when trying to apply groupwork in practice and the fourth section of the questionnaire concerned the potential needs of mental health practitioners *who did* apply groupwork in their practice.

Method

Sampling

A range of mental health practitioners were contacted and sent an information sheet explaining the study and a copy of the survey questionnaire. Practitioners were contacted via an NHS website directory of adult mental health services in the South London and Maudsley NHS Trust (SLAM). A total of 920 questionnaires were sent to a total of 132 services in four main 'boroughs' comprising the SLAM NHS trust (Croydon, 19 services; Lambeth, 54 services; Lewisham, 27 services and Southwark, 32 services). Borough based services were not contacted if the description of the services provided on the website or by the service manager clearly precluded

the option of groupwork use in those services (e.g. 'rapid response' crisis assessment/intervention teams, neuropsychiatry assessment clinics etc). All other services were contacted initially by telephone. Service managers/coordinators were contacted and given a brief summary of the study and asked if they considered it appropriate for team members to be sent copies of the information sheet and questionnaire. Only one service declined to receive information sheets and questionnaires. Team managers/coordinators were sent batches of between 10 and 20 questionnaires and asked to distribute these to team members. Covering letters requested that the questionnaire packs be distributed equally among mental health professionals in their team (including psychologists, psychiatrists, occupational therapists, mental health nurses and social workers). The covering letters also requested that the questionnaires be distributed both to team members who had been involved in groupwork and team members who had not been involved in groupwork.

Questionnaire design

The survey questionnaire contained 71 statements about groupwork with 'Likert-type' scale responses for each question. An example of the likert type response format as illustrated in Figure 1 overleaf.

This scale differed from traditional scale responses in that the response '5. Don't know' was set to the right, away from the main body of the response options, rather than between response 2 and response 3. This was done in order to minimise the likelihood of default 'don't know' responses. The 71 questions were divided into a number of sections that referred to the four main domains of the investigation (client-orientated groupwork goals, methods of groupwork, obstacles to the delivery of groupwork and needs of practitioners offering groupwork). In addition approximately half of the questions were designed to be completed by mental health practitioners who had offered groupwork over the previous 12 months (Sections E, F and G) and the other half of the questionnaire was designed to be completed by those who had not offered groupwork over the previous 12-month period (Section A, B and C). Two additional sections, each comprising a single item were

Figure 1

An example of the Likert-type scale response format to question 13

13. It would be difficult to fit in working with groups into my existing workload.

1. Strongly disagree	2. Disagree	3. Agree	4. Strongly agree		5. Don't know

directed at those who had offered groupwork over the past 12 months (Section D 'Assuming you have been involved in groupwork during the last year, please indicate in what capacity by ticking the box next to the item that applies to you' and section H 'while offering groupwork, have you received specialised groupwork consultation/supervision on a regular basis during the last year'.

Furthermore, all respondents regardless of groupwork involvement over the previous 12-month period were required to complete a final section (I) including three questions about the need for regular supervision for working with groups, whether specialist training for working with groups had been provided, and the perceived need for specialised training. All respondents were required to read an initial information sheet and to complete a cover page that included directions on how to complete the questionnaire. In addition the initial section contained a series of questions relating to profession, length of working since qualification, diagnostic categories of the clients served by the respondents' team and whether or not groupwork had been offered by the respondent.

The survey aimed to collect the views of mental health professionals regarding the viable goals of groupwork. This aspect of the survey was conceptualised within a 'quality of life' framework. Groupwork practitioners and mental health professionals who had and had not offered groupwork were asked to rate the capacity of groupwork to affect a range of areas that would be expected to contribute to client 'quality of life' (e.g. positive self concept, social relations, health, living conditions, financial concerns (Oliver et al., 1996).

The second aspect of the questionnaire sought to obtain the views of mental health professionals regarding the applicability of the major approaches to groupwork to the clients served by their teams. For example, did groupwork practitioners subscribe to particular models of groupwork over others? Were behavioural/ cognitive approaches seen as important approaches to use when delivering groupwork and if so were these approaches seen as more useful than other approaches? The third aspect of the survey related to obstacles faced by mental health practitioners when trying to apply groupwork in practice. Statements to be rated included possible concerns about the effectiveness of groupwork, client take-up and client engagement, possible lack of supervision and workload involved in setting up new groups.

The fourth section of the questionnaire concerned the potential needs of mental health practitioners *who did* apply groupwork in their practice, with regard to the need for specialised training in groupwork.

Results

Description of the sample obtained

Respondents

157 mental health professionals participated in the current study by returning completed survey questionnaires over a 4-month period (a 17% response rate). Some practitioners' questionnaires had not been completed correctly so data from a total of 155 practitioners was included in the analysis, giving a final 16.8% response rate.

Professions responding

Provisional counts of staff in mental health teams in the London area were compiled as part of the Mental Health Service Mapping Exercise for 2002 (Glover & Barnes, 2001). Analysis of this preliminary data allows the numbers in a given profession responding to the current study to be expressed as a percentage of the total number working in the given profession in the different borough-based regions, as recorded in the service mapping database. This analysis indicated that approximately 38% of psychiatrists responded to the current study, together with 33%

of nurses, 59% of occupational therapists, 38% of social workers and 80% of psychologists.

In addition, the range of professionals responding had varied lengths of professional experience ranging from over thirty years in the NHS to just embarking on training courses, see Figure 2 below.

What psychiatric conditions were seen by respondents?

Each practitioner was asked 'What is the diagnostic category of most clients served by your team?' The single largest category was psychotic difficulties (32.2%), with neurotic difficulties coming second (13.0%) and personality disorders third (0.7%).

However, more often than not teams did not concentrate on any one psychiatric category – 54.0% of the respondents described their teams as dealing with a mixed range of psychiatric categories, of which the combination of psychotic difficulties , neurotic difficulties and personality disorder was the largest (19.2% of the sample).

Opinions about the client orientated goals of groupwork

Mental health professionals who were involved in offering groupwork to clients rated their level of agreement/disagreement with a number of statements about the possible goals of groupwork. The mean levels of agreement to a series of statements about goals were ranked in order of agreement (see Table 1.)

'Enhancing clients' positive self-concept' was the goal which attracted the strongest practitioners agreement. By comparison, these practitioners agreed least with the goal of helping clients with legal matters. In between was a mix of medical and social goals. While helping clients cope with symptoms came second, expanding clients' social relations came third. So – although most practitioners came from professions affiliated to medicine the goals they identified for groupwork were far wider than those concerned with strictly psychiatric conditions.

To test the hypothesis that the responses to questions about groupwork goals (Table 1) varied significantly across the 12 'goals' questions, a Friedman Test was conducted on the responses of

Figure 2

Mean years since qualifying by profession ('other' = counsellors, psychotherapists, support workers)

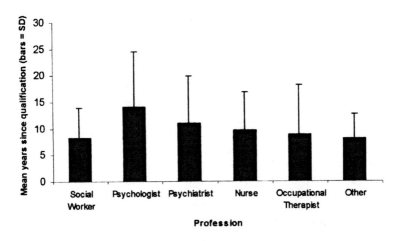

practitioners who had offered groupwork. The ratings given by practitioners to questions about goals varied significantly across the 12 questions (X^2 = 320.304, df = 11, $p < 0.0001$).

In order to investigate the possibility that quality of life goals 'clustered' or 'grouped' together in terms of practitioners responses to particular items, the responses from all practitioners to all questions were subjected to principal components analysis. This analysis allows a large number of responses to be measured so that we can investigate whether responses represent a smaller number of *dimensions or factors*. A dimension would consist of different questions which had been answered in a similar way by each practitioner. The responses of both practitioners who had and who had not offered groupwork were included for the purposes of the factor analysis. On this occasion, three components with an eigenvalue of greater than 1.0 were found; the scree plot also indicated three components. The components and the variables that load on them are shown in Table 2.

Table 2 indicates that practitioners' responses to questions

Table 1
The views of professionals regarding the possible quality of life goals.

Statement	Mean	(SD)
Enhancing clients' positive self concept	3.40	(.49)
Helping clients cope with symptoms	3.38	(.50)
Expanding clients' social relations	3.32	(.50)
Promoting clients' health	3.29	(.49)
Increasing clients' work and education opportunities	3.08	(.55)
Improving clients' family relations	3.07	(.56)
Alleviating the burden on clients' carers	3.02	(.52)
Removing underlying causes of clients' symptoms	2.87	(.70)
Improving clients' living conditions	2.81	(.67)
Improving clients' financial situation	2.59	(.60)
Enhancing clients' involvement in their own religious concerns	2.58	(.65)
Helping clients with legal matters	2.48	(.59)

Items listed in descending order of agreement. This means higher levels of agreement with statements at the head of the table progressing towards lower levels of agreement with statements at the foot (1: strongly disagree, 2: disagree, 3: agree, 4: strongly agree).

grouped into three components comprising clusters of different questions. The first component we called 'social psychiatry' as it included a number of psychiatric and social goals. The second component was labelled 'daily living with the family' because it included practical goals such as finance, living conditions, carer burden and family relations. The third component included questions that related to goals that were of a wider or more long-term nature (such as work, education and religious concerns).

Opinions about the possible approaches to use in groupwork

Inspection of Table 3 indicates that no groupwork approach was totally rejected by all practitioners. The range of *possible* responses

Table 2
The goals of groupwork: The components found by the principal components analysis and the variables that load on them.

Component 1 *Social Psychiatry* (Morgan, 1993)	Component 2 *Daily living with family* (Lefley & Wascow, 1994)	Component 3 Life-long goals
Q.B27: Expanding clients' social relations.	Q. B23: Improving clients' financial situation.	Q. B21: Increasing clients' work and education opportunities.
Q. B28: Promoting clients' health.	Q. B24: Improving clients living conditions.	Q. B22: Enhancing clients' involvement in their own religious
Q. B29: Enhancing clients' positive self-concept.	Q. B30: Alleviating burden on clients' carers.	
Q. B31: Helping clients cope with symptoms.		

was divided between 1–2 for disagreement and 3-4 for agreement. Yet, the findings show that no average fell below the score of 2.

Still, some approaches won stronger support than others. Table 3 shows that the most favoured place was accorded *equally* to two approaches: 'Facilitating spontaneous interaction among clients in the group', and 'Combining the modification of clients' behaviour with changing their thoughts and beliefs' (cognitive behavioural). On the other hand, practitioners favoured least the approach of 'Staging make believe episodes during which clients enact their conflict situations' (enactment methods). However, it is worth noting that the average of responses for this approach included variation in the standard deviation of the mean of individuals' responses. This indicated that practitioners disagreed among themselves more widely. Psychodramatic methods (such as staging make-believe episodes) appear to be controversial for this sample of

Table 3: The views of professionals regarding approaches to use in groupwork.

Statement	Mean	(SD)
Combining the modification of the clients behaviour with changing their thoughts and beliefs	3.15	(.62)
Facilitating spontaneous interaction among clients in the group	3.15	(.56)
Modifying clients' behaviour	3.11	(.53)
Helping clients to deal with other professions in meeting their medical, financial and/or practical needs.	2.96	(.54)
Challenging thoughts and beliefs	2.96	(.63)
Encouraging clients to help and support one another outside of the group	2.92	(.72)
Eliciting clients unconscious preoccupations and interpreting these	2.47	(.74)
Mobilising clients to form pressure groups that lobby organisations in pursuit of clients' rights.	2.38	(.62)
Staging make believe episodes during which clients enact their own conflict situations	2.34	(.82)

Items listed in descending mean 'order of agreement' high level of agreement with statements at the head of the table progressing towards low level of agreement with statements at the foot (1: strongly disagree, 2: disagree, 3: agree, 4: strongly agree).

practitioners. Accounting for the standard deviation in the level of agreement, 4 statements consistently yielded ratings of agreement that remained above the mid-point of 2.5. On average, practitioners agreed with the statement that groupwork *helped clients to deal with other professions in meeting their medical, financial and/or practical needs*. They also agreed with the statement that *modifying clients' behaviour* was an approach that they 'might prefer'.

To test the hypothesis that the responses to questions about groupwork approaches (Table 3.) varied significantly across the 9 'approaches' questions, a Friedman Test was conducted on the responses of practitioners. The ratings given by practitioners to questions about approaches varied significantly across the 9 questions (χ^2 = 145.613, df = 8, p < 0.0001).

Again, in order to further investigate the degree to which questions within sections about approaches to offering groupwork grouped together on the basis of practitioners' responses to them, the data were analysed by means of a principal components analysis, with varimax rotation. The responses of practitioners who had and who had not offered groupwork were combined for the purposes of the factor analysis. Three components with an eigenvalue of greater than 1.0 were found; the scree plot also indicated 3 components. The components and the variables that load on them are shown in Table 4 overleaf which demonstrates that the responses of practitioners to questions concerning groupwork approaches clustered into three main components. These were labelled 'social groupwork', 'cognitive behaviour therapy' and 'group psychotherapy'.

How did professionals view the obstacles to offering groupwork?

Average ratings indicated that respondents agreed with statements about *workload demands* making it difficult to offer groupwork (see Table 5). In addition, responses indicated that many of those not offering groupwork felt that they did not know enough about working with groups. In contrast, respondents who had not offered groupwork did not, on average, agree with items about groupwork not meeting the needs of the clients served and agreed with statements about the effectiveness of the approach being sufficiently established.

A Friedman Test was conducted on the responses of practitioners who had offered groupwork and the ratings given by practitioners to questions about obstacles were found to vary significantly across the 12 questions (χ^2 = 40.189, df=11, p<0.0001).

What helped those who were involved in offering groupwork?

The majority of practitioners who had offered groupwork in their practice produced mean rating levels above the midpoint on the 4-point scale of 2.5 (see Table 6). The ratings assigned to questions about what helped them offer groupwork were

Table 4

Possible approaches to groupwork: The components found by the principal components analysis and the variables that load on them.

Component 1 Social Groupwork (Brown 1992; Doel & Sawdon, 1999)	Component 2 Cognitive behaviour therapy (Scott & Stradling, 1988)	Component 3 Group psychotherapy (Mackenzie 1997; Yalom, 1995; Foulks, 1964; Stock-Whitaker, 2001)
Q.C38: Encouraging clients to help and support one another outside of the group.	Q. C35: Changing clients' thoughts and beliefs	Q. C41: Facilitating spontaneous interaction among clients in the group.
Q.C39: Helping clients to deal with other professionals in meeting their medical, financial or practical needs.	Q. C36: Modifying clients' behaviour	Q. C42: Eliciting client's unconscious preoccupations and interpreting these.
Q. C40: Mobilising clients to form pressure groups that lobby organisations in pursuit of clients' rights	Q. C37: Combining the modification of the clients' behaviour with changing their thoughts and beliefs.	
Q. C43: Staging make-believe episodes in which clients enact their own conflict situations.		

subjected to a Friedman Test which indicated that ratings given by practitioners varied significantly across the twelve questions. Average ratings indicated that respondents agreed with statements about *groupwork being relevant to the needs of the clients served*. In addition, results indicated that many of those offering groupwork *did not think using groupwork would have a potentially negative effect upon the clients they worked with*. Furthermore, mean ratings of agreement above the midpoint were assigned to items relating to the effectiveness of groupwork. Practitioners agreed with the

Table 5
The views of professionals who did not offer groupwork regarding possible obstacles

Statement	Mean	(SD)
Groupwork is too difficult to fit into my existing workload	2.97	(.68)
The rate of clients not taking up the offer of groupwork or dropping out of it is too high	2.47	(.54)
I don't know enough about working with groups	2.39	(.70)
No supervision will be available if groupwork is offered	2.39	(.77)
Others in my team are offering this service	2.37	(.81)
It is too difficult to properly engage so many clients within one group	2.37	(.59)
Too much work is involved in setting up a new group	2.35	(.51)
Nobody else in my team seems to be interested in offering groupwork	2.27	(.61)
Groupwork may have a negative effect on the clients served	2.1	(.62)
It is impossible to incorporate groupwork within the demands of the care programme approach	2.1	(.57)
The effectiveness of groupwork is not sufficiently established	2.04	(.67)
Groupwork would not meet the need of the clients served by our team	1.97	(.58)

Items listed in descending mean 'order of agreement' high level of agreement with statements at the head of the table progressing towards low level of agreement with statements at the foot (1: strongly disagree, 2: disagree, 3: agree, 4: strongly agree).

statement that the *effectiveness had been sufficiently established*, and that *others in their team were already offering the service.*

The need for training

Finally, findings from the section of the questionnaire (Section I) relating to the perceived need for specialised training, in relation to having received it, were not significant. Inspection of Figure 3 indicated that most of the sample never received specialised training in groupwork, yet a larger proportion indicated that they felt they needed such specialised training.

The data suggest a slight tendency on the part of those who had received such training to agree with the need for it, and for those who never had received it, to disagree with such need, but there was no statistically significant relationship between the rated necessity of specialised training and whether or not training had been received ($\chi2 = .735$, $df = 1$, $p > 0.05$).

Discussion

The major findings can be summarised as follows:

- The professional experience of these practitioners varied considerably: from over thirty years to the newly qualified.
- The psychiatric conditions these practitioners treated were largely mixed, but the single largest group was of patients suffering from psychotic difficulties.
- Enhancing clients' positive self-concept was the quality of life goal which attracted the strongest agreement from practitioners.
- Three types of quality of life goals were identified: social psychiatry, daily life with the family and life-long goals.
- The quality of life goals were pursued through different groupwork methods, with 'Facilitating spontaneous interaction among clients in the group' and 'Combining the modification of clients' behaviour with changing their thoughts and beliefs' being most favoured.
- No particular groupwork method was rejected, but three

Table 6
The views of professionals who did offer groupwork regarding what helped them to offer the service.

Statement	Mean	(SD)
Groupwork was relevant to the needs of the clients served	3.53	(.73)
Groupwork was not thought to have a potentially negative effect upon the clients served	3.22	(.65)
The effectiveness of groupwork was significantly established	3.17	(.60)
Others in my team were offering this service	3.03	(.65)
The amount of work involved in setting up a new group was acceptable	2.98	(.55)
It was possible to incorporate groupwork within the demands of the care program approach	2.98	(.64)
I felt I knew enough about working with groups	2.89	(.59)
The rate of clients not taking up this service or dropping out was acceptable	2.74	(.70)
It would not be too difficult to fit in working with groups into my existing workload.	2.74	(.83)
It was not too difficult to properly engage so many clients within one group	2.73	(.70)
Others in my team were interested in offering groupwork	2.72	(.87)
Supervision was available when groupwork was offered.	2.52	(.78)

Items listed in descending mean 'order of agreement' high level of agreement with statements at the head of the table progressing towards low level of agreement with statements at the foot (1: strongly disagree, 2: disagree, 3: agree, 4: strongly agree). Friedman test: $\chi^2 = 40.209$, df = 11, p < 0.000.

Figure 3
Perceived necessity of specialised training in relation to training received

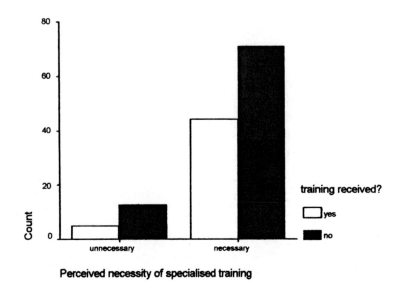

Perceived necessity of specialised training

'camps' appeared to exist: Cognitive Behavioural, Social Group Work, and Group Psychotherapy.

- Conviction about the merit of groupwork may be the most important issue that helps practitioners to become involved in the practice of groupwork.
- The size and the nature of their caseload may be the most important hindrance to practitioners getting involved in groupwork, followed by lack of training and supervision.
- Specialised training in groupwork is wanted but is not available as much as is needed.

Surveys of the type reported here are open to bias and the distortions arising out of non-returns can be a major factor contributing to bias. This survey achieved a response rate of only 17% and as such the findings reported here should be interpreted with caution. Mental health professionals often do not have the time to complete all postal surveys sent to them. The operating bias in response is likely to be toward those who work more regularly with groups and are committed to the advancement of groupwork training and practice. One possible interpretation of these findings is that the views of a small number of experienced and committed groupwork practitioners are represented here, and as such, no generalisations regarding the state of groupwork practice in NHS mental health teams can be drawn. However, in response to this criticism, analyses of the responses would indicate that roughly similar numbers of practitioners who had never offered groupwork responded as did practitioners who had offered groupwork. This would indicate that within the context of a low response rate overall, there was no marked bias toward practitioners who had offered groupwork. Furthermore, it is clear from the limited analysis of the type of mental health professionals returning questionnaires that, with the exception of psychologists, a roughly equal proportion of mental health workers responded to the study, when response rates were expressed as a proportion of the total number of professionals in a given field working in the areas surveyed.

The current project has sought to collect initial data regarding the views of mental health practitioners who have and have not offered groupwork in their practice. The findings would indicate that those who do not offer groupwork currently believe that a groupwork approach would meet the needs of the clients served by their teams, that its effectiveness is sufficiently established and that it could be incorporated into the care program approach. Those who did not offer groupwork did not seem to be opposed to groupwork in principle. However, existing workload issues appeared to constitute the main impediment to working in this way. Of the practitioners who did offer the service, all those responding either agreed or strongly agreed that groupwork was relevant to the needs of the clients served, that it would not have a damaging effect on clients, and that the effectiveness of the approach had been sufficiently established.

In terms of the possible goals of groupwork, practitioners believed most strongly that groupwork should be used to enhance client's self-concept, help clients cope with symptoms and promote health, expand their social relations, increase their work and education opportunities and improve client's family relations (while alleviating the burden on carers). The scope of groupwork practice, as envisaged by those who currently offer the service is therefore quite broad. Favoured approaches to use were cognitive/ behavioural in orientation, but also emphasised the need to facilitate spontaneous interaction among clients in the group.

In order to generate possible questions for further research, factor analysis of survey responses was carried out in the current study. The results of this factor analysis produced a number of components in the separate sections of the questionnaire relating to the obstacles to using groupwork, the goals of groupwork, and possible approaches to use when offering groupwork. We have provisionally named these components in line with the variables that load on them (see Tables 2 and 4).

Responses to questions in the section on approaches to groupwork (see Table 4) elicited three main components. The first of these was a 'social groupwork' component, which emphasised the usefulness of groupwork in engendering support between clients when attempting to meet their needs. The variables related to interpersonal relationships in the context of meeting needs, supporting one another, mobilising each other in pursuit of rights and so on. The second component emphasised cognitive behavioural variables such as helping clients to modify their behaviour and change their thoughts and beliefs. The third component involved the facilitation of spontaneous interactions with clients in combination with interpreting clients' unconscious preoccupations. That third component emphasised the importance of interaction within the group that was not explicitly goal orientated but rather spontaneous and dynamic within the group. It would appear that effective group working may need to incorporate direct therapy orientated interventions in the context of building important spontaneous and goal-directed interpersonal skills.

Responses to questions concerning the possible of goals of groupwork contributed to three possible components (see Table 2.). The first of these related to the goals of social psychiatric interventions. Variables loading on this component included items about health concerns and symptoms in conjunction with clients' social relationships. The second component related to more client-orientated family concerns including the financial situation of clients, their living conditions and 'carer burden'. The third addressed more long-term concerns including work, education and religious concerns.

The current findings relate to the views of mental health professionals in one large mental health trust in London. It is suggested that this study should be replicated in other large cities in the UK with the aim of building a more complete picture about the use of groupwork in mental health teams in the UK. In addition, the current study has implications for the training of practitioners in the provision of groupwork. There was a clearly communicated lack of specialised training for working with groups and the majority of respondents believed such training to be necessary in the context of an NHS trust in which groupwork played an important role.

References

Ashbach, C. and Schermer, V.L. (1987) *Object Relations, the Self, and the Group: A conceptual paradigm.* London: Routledge & Kegan Paul

Blatner, H.S.A. (1973) *Acting In: Practical applications of psychodramatic techniques.* New York: Springer

Brandler, S. and Roman, C. P. (1991) *Group Work: Skills and strategies for effective interventions.* New York: The Howarth Press

Brown, A. (1992) *Groupwork.* 3rd Edition. Aldershot: Ashgate

Brown, N.W. (1998) *Psycho-Educational Groups.* Bristol: Taylor and Francis

Cowburn, M. (2000) Consultancy to groupwork programmes for adult male sex offenders: Some reflections on knowledge and processes. *British Journal of Social Work,* 30, 635-648

Darnley-Smith, R. and Patey, H.M. (2003) *Music Therapy.* London: Sage

Daste, B.M. (1990) Important considerations in groupwork with cancer patients. *Social Work with Groups,* 13, 69-81

Department of Health (1997) *Directory of Community Mental Health Training, 1997.* London: The Mental Health Foundation

Doel, M. and Sawdon, C. (1999) *The Essential Groupworker.* London: Jessica Kingsley

Doel, M. and Sawdon, C. (2000) No group is an island: Groupwork in a social work agency. in O. Manor (ed.) *Ripples: Groupwork in different settings.* (pp.65-84) London: Whiting and Birch

Doel, M. and Sawdon, C. (2001) What makes for successful groupwork? A survey of agencies in the UK. *British Journal of Social Work*, 31, 437-463

Foulks, S.H. (1964) *Therapeutic Group Analysis*. London: George Allen and Unwin

Foulks, S.H. (1975) *Group Analytic Psychotherapy*. London: Gordon and Breach

Free, M. (1999) *Cognitive Therapy in Groups*. Chichester: Wiley

Gitterman, A. and Shulman, L. (Eds.) (1994) *Mutual Aid Groups: Vulnerable populations and the life cycle*. 2nd Edition. New York: Columbia University Press,

Glover, G. and Barnes, D. (2001) Mental health service provision for working age adults in England 2001 – www.dur.ac.uk/service.mapping. University of Durham Centre for Public Mental Health

Gotlib, I.H. and Hammen, C.L. (1992) *Psychological Aspects of Depression: Toward a cognitive-interpersonal integration*. Chichester: Wiley

Harris, N., Williams, S. and Bradshaw, T. (eds.) (2002) *Psychosocial Interventions for People with Schizophrenia*. Basingstoke: Palgrave

Lefley, H.P. and Wascow, M. (eds.) (1994) *Helping Families Cope with Mental Illness*. Harwood : Academic Press

Macgowan, M.J. (2000) Evaluation of a measure of engagement for group work. *Research on Social Work in Practice*, 10, 348-361

MacKenzie, K.R. (1997) *Time-Managed Group Psychotherapy: Effective clinical applications*. London: American Psychiatric Press

Manor, O. (2000a) Help as mutual aid: Groupwork in mental health. in O. Manor (Ed.) *Ripples: Groupwork in different settings*. London: Whiting and Birch, pp.85-104

Manor, O. (2000b) *Choosing a Groupwork Approach: An inclusive stance*. London: Jessica Kingsley

Manor, O. (2000c) The working alliance.in M. Davis (Ed.) *The Blackwell Encyclopaedia of Social Work*. (pp.375-576) Oxford: Blackwell

Manor, O. (2003) Groupwork fit for purpose? An inclusive framework for mental health. *Groupwork*, 13, 3, 49-76

Martin, M.A., & Nayowith, S.A. (1988) Creating community – group work to develop social support networks with homeless mentally ill. *Social Work with Groups*. 11, 79-93

Meekums, B. (2002) *Dance Movement Therapy*. London: Sage

Moreno, J.L. (1964) *Psychodrama*. New York: Beacon Press

Morgan, S. (1993) *Community Mental Health: Practical approaches to long term problems*. London: Chapman & Hall

Mullender, A. and Ward, D. (1991) *Self-directed Groupwork: Users take action for empowerment*. London: Whiting and Birch

Oliver, H. (1999) How to use quality of life measures in individual care. In: S. Priebe, J.P.L. Oliver, N.S.W. Kaiser (eds.) *Quality of Life and Mental Health Care*. (pp.82-105) Petersfield: Wrightson Biomedical

Oliver, J., Huxley, P., Bridges, K. and Mohamad, H. (1996) *Quality of Life and Mental Health Services*. London: Routledge

Oliver, N., Carson, J., Missenden, K., Towey, A., Dunn, L., Collins, E., and Holloway, F. (1996) Assessing the quality of life of the long-term mentally ill: A comparative measure of two studies. *International Journal of Methods in Psychiatric Research*, 6, 161-166

Onyett, S. (2003) *Team Working in Mental Health*. Basingstoke: Palgrave

Payne, M. (2000) *Teamwork in Multiprofessional Care*. Basingstoke: Palgrave

Phillips, J. (2001) *Groupwork in Social Care*. London: Jessica Kingsley

Platzer, H., Blake, D., and Ashford, D. (2000) Barriers to learning from reflection: A study of the use of groupwork with post-registration nurses. *Journal of Advanced Nursing*, 31, 1001-1008

Priebe, S., Oliver, J.P.L. and Kaiser, W. (1999) *Quality of Life and Mental Health Care*. Petersfield: Wrightson Biomedical Pub

Pugh, J. (1995) Groupwork with HIV-Positive drug misusers in prison. *Irish Journal of Psychological Medicine*, 12, 12-16

Rogers, C. (1971) *Encounter Groups*. London: Allen Lane the Penguin Press

Rose, S. D. (1977) *Group Therapy: A behavioral approach*. Englewood Cliffs, NJ: Prentice Hall

Rose, S. D. (1980) *A Casebook in Behavioral Therapy*. Englewood Cliffs, NJ: Prentice Hall

Schermer, V.L. and Pines, M. (eds.) (1999) *Group Psychotherapy of the Psychoses*. London: Jessica Kingsley

Schwartz, W. (1976) Between client and system: The mediating function. In: R.W. Roberts and H. Northern, (Eds.) *Theories of Social Work with Groups*. (pp.171-197) New York: Columbia University press

Scott, M.J. and Stradling, S.G. (1998) *Brief Group Counselling*. Chichester: Wiley

Shaw, E.M., Corsini, R.J., Blake, R.R. and Mouton, J.S. (1980) *Role Playing: A Practical Manual for Group Facilitators*. San Diego CA: California University Press

Shulman, L. (1999) *The Skills of Helping Individuals, Families, groups, and communities*. Itasca, IL: Peacock Pub

Stock-Whitaker, D. (2001) *Using Groups to Help People*. Hove: Brunner-Routledge

Training Organisation for the Personal Social Services (2002) *The National Occupational Standards for Social Work*. London: TOPPS

Trower, P., Bryant, B. and Argyle, M. (1978) *Social Skills and Mental Health*. London: Methuen

Waller, D. and Gilroy, A. (1992) *Art Therapy: A handbook*. Milton Keynes: Open University Press

Watson, G., Scott, C., Ragalsky, S. (1996) Refusing to be marginalized: Groupwork in mental health services for women survivors of childhood sexual abuse. *Journal of Community and Applied Social Psychology*, 6, 341-354

Whitaker, D.S. and Lieberman, M. (1964) *Psychotherapy Through the Group Process*. London: Routledge and Kegan Paul

Yalom, I. D. (1995) *The Theory and Practice of Group Psychotherapy*. 4th Edition. New York: Basic Books

This chapter was first published in 2003 in *Groupwork* Vol. 13(3), pp.6-36

At the time of writing:
Ben Papps was Lecturer in Clinical Psychology, Institute of Psychiatry, London.
Oded Manor was Principal Lecturer in Social Work, Middlesex University, Enfield.
Jerome Carson was Senior Lecturer in Clinical Psychology, Institute of Psychiatry, London

Groupwork with schizophrenia: Clinical aspects

Susan E. Mason[1]

Summary: *This is a review of the clinical aspects of using groups to help people who have schizophrenia. The latest research and clinical data show groups to be effective in enhancing the quality of life for patients and supporting their recovery from the acute effects of the disease. Groupwork is shown to contribute to: 1) helping patients cope with the positive, negative and disorganisation symptoms; 2) providing first episode patients with their special needs; 3) monitoring patients who are participating in research; and 4) working with patients' racial and ethnic differences. Clinical vignettes from practice in the US are used to illustrate treatment issues but there are references to how these may apply to groupwork in the UK and elsewhere.*

Key words: *schizophrenia; quality of life; symptoms*

Introduction

Patients who have schizophrenia present a formidable challenge even to the most experienced clinicians. They are difficult to treat because they have complex symptoms and their needs are varied. Clinicians who use groups for patients with schizophrenia have, in the past, been mostly on their own with little guidance from the literature, but researchers in the treatment of the disease are now recognising the value of group interventions. This article focuses on four critical aspects of schizophrenia treatment that can be effectively accomplished in groups:

1. helping patients cope with the positive, negative, and disorganisation symptoms;
2. providing for the special needs of patients in the first episode of schizophrenia;
3. helping patients gain the most advantages from participating in research studies; and
4. working with patients' racial and ethnic differences.

The discussion is grounded in the latest research and the author's hospital-based experience with schizophrenia in the United States. The emphasis is on what we now know about schizophrenia and how groups can help patients live more productive lives.

An overview

On-going research on schizophrenia, its symptoms, course and outcome is impacting on how patients are being treated. New medications are now bringing patients to higher levels of functioning and increased expectations for quality of life gains. Patients are requesting treatments that will allow them to regain at least a portion of the lifestyle they knew before they became ill. Groups also serve to help patients get the most benefits from research participation and are a way to address racial and ethnic differences. Groupwork is increasingly viewed as an overall successful therapy that helps patients cope with the debilitating aspects of the illness and improves their day-to-day functioning.

The symptoms of schizophrenia, positive, negative and disorganisation, can be managed well in groups. The positive symptoms are delusions and hallucinations, the psychological phenomena that clinicians expect to see in patients with schizophrenia. The difficult-to-treat negative symptoms include avolition (apathy), alogia (poverty of speech), anhedonia (lack of pleasure) and flat affect. Negative symptoms, found in many patients after the positive symptoms have fully or partially remitted, do not always respond to medications and anti-psychotic medications can make them appear worse. Symptoms of disorganisation include inappropriate affect, disorganised behaviour, and disorganised speech. Patients with disorganisation symptoms may laugh at sad experiences, have accelerated or extremely slowed movements and often have difficult-to-understand speech, all of which makes them appear odd (Barlow & Durand, 1999). Disorganisation is often overlooked when acute positive or intractable negative symptoms require a great deal of attention. However, being disorganised contributes to social isolation, a serious problem for patients who very much need emotional support from others. Most patients experience all or combinations of positive, negative and disorganisation symptoms at different stages of the illness. Groups are effective for recognising symptoms and developing helpful coping strategies.

Groupwork with patients in the first episode of schizophrenia is now being recognised as an important way to serve this special needs population. In many agencies, first episode schizophrenia patients are placed in the same groups with those who are more chronic. The reason for this is often economic; agencies cannot afford to run separate programs. Many clinicians believe that although first episode patients are likely to be younger, psychosocial interventions for both newly diagnosed and long-term patients are sufficiently similar to treat them together. In contrast to this position, there are a growing number of advocates for separate groups for first episode patients where the focus is on the newness of the illness (Edwards, France, McGorry & Jackson, 1994; Hogarty, et. al., 1997; Miller & Mason, 1998; 1999). These advocates believe that patients experience the first episode as so traumatic that they require specialised attention, and that separate groups are well suited for their clinical needs.

Participation in research is a subject that engenders heated discussions. Those who oppose it, argue that schizophrenia causes diminished capacity to fully understand the risks of research participation. Those in favour cite the numerous advances that clinical research has brought to schizophrenia treatment. Both sides agree that research participants need to understand protocols and have the safest possible care (Mason, Bermanzohn & Siris, 1998). In response to this controversy, there are now focused efforts to ensure that protocols and consent forms are understood (Brabbins, Butler, & Bentall, 1996). Group therapy is recognised as an effective vehicle for enhancing patients' understanding of protocols and reducing risks by allowing clinicians to monitor patient progress.

Groups are also helpful for managing issues related to racial and ethnic differences, a neglected aspect of clinical treatment. The group is a safe place for patients to express and work on their feelings about their prejudices. The experience of being in group brings to its members a feeling of community and cohesion that works against racism and ethnic enmity.

Groups are also effective for increasing levels of social adjustment when they include social skills training. This use of group increases patients' feelings of personal well being and is most helpful when the age of onset for schizophrenia is earlier than twenty-four (Marder, et al., 1996).

There are many other ways to appreciate the value of the group experience for people who have schizophrenia. The group can be viewed as a family substitute where a caring atmosphere is encouraged (Munich, 1997). It may be seen as place where patients are helped to make both treatment and personal decisions, and where leaders have the opportunity to guide and direct. Group leaders can help patients with focusing on issues, making decisions about their education, vocational plans and relationships with family and friends. It is the leader's role to ascertain the level at which group members can comprehend these issues and utilise the group process at the members' level and pace. Sometimes patients relapse and then must leave a group, which sometimes happens regardless of how well treatment is conducted (Lieberman, 1993). When this happens, the group processes the loss with members expressing their feelings about not seeing Jimmy or Mary in group and their own fears about the possibility of relapse and anger about having the disease. Expressing and processing these feelings helps build a sense of community and adds to the understanding the course of the illness (Miller & Mason, 1998).

The pervasive use of group treatment for schizophrenia patients continues even when there is a mix of opinion on whether they can benefit (Scott & Stradling, 1998). Most experts agree that the classic developmental stages of group (Garland & Kolodny, 1973) do not apply. These stages (re-affiliation, power and control; intimacy;

differentiation and separation) are not typically experienced by patients who are struggling to maintain their grasp of reality. There may be exceptions, such as patients who are well along in their recovery and are more able than others to experience differentiation and separation, but the nature of the illness with its ongoing struggle with reality precludes making this an expectation (Miller & Mason, 1998).

Treatment settings

Group treatment for schizophrenia is found in a variety of settings and utilises several different models. Bond and De Graaf-Kaiser (1990) provide a detailed discussion of group treatment approaches that are applicable for schizophrenia. Settings that are most commonly used today include:

1. inpatient and day-hospitals;
2. clinics and day-treatment programs;
3. research groups in psychiatric facilities;
4. outreach programs; and
5. multi-setting continuity of care programs.

Inpatient and day-hospital groups are typically short-term and open to members when their symptoms are severe enough to require hospital treatment. Group members are at about the same level of acuity in their symptom and functioning presentations. They learn about the illness in group psychoeducation sessions and discuss their personal experiences of having the disease. The emphasis is on supportive rather than on insight therapy (Kanas, 1996; Kates & Rockland, 1994; Yalum, 1983). These residential and day hospital groups are common in North America and Western Europe, but they have received relatively little attention in the treatment literature.

Clinic and day-treatment groups, meeting once or twice a week, serve patients as part of an overall treatment plan that typically includes medication. Groups help the clinician monitor medication and overall treatment compliance. Patients are helped from becoming overly isolated and members receive social service and health-care advice with referrals to medical clinics, as needed. The reports on these groups are largely positive and they are viewed as important therapeutic components of treatment (Kopelowicz & Liberman, 1998).

Research groups take place in a variety of milieus. They are set apart by exclusive membership criteria based on study protocols. The staff/patient ratios are high and allow for more attention to each participant. Study group members often feel a sense of pride and enhanced status in knowing they are participating in important projects. Hogarty et al. (1997) writes extensively on studies for schizophrenia treatment that includes group treatment. His research staff consistently find that groups increase positive outcomes in medication studies by providing social support and patient education.

Community outreach groups meet in homeless shelters, drug treatment agencies, store-front community agencies, and a variety of mental health and community based organisations. Clubhouses use a rehabilitation model that separates the group experience from psychiatric treatment. The emphasis is on social and daily living skills training, pursuing practical needs, and psychoeducation. These groups appear to be helpful in preventing re-hospitalisations and getting patients the services they need (Edwards et al., 1994; Scott & Dixon, 1995) but just as important, they provide comfort for many who are homeless or live in transient or chaotic settings.

Continuity of care teams follow patients as they move through the various levels of psychiatric service (Essock & Kontos, 1995). As patients move from an inpatient unit to day treatment, and then to the outpatient clinic, they participate in groups often led by the same group leader. If there is a need to return to a higher level of service, the group at that level is familiar to the returning patient so there is a greater continuity in the treatment. Unfortunately, there are few descriptions of how these groups function (Miller & Mason, 1999).

Groupwork with schizophrenia

Clinicians are often faced with the dilemma of wanting to treat patients using the most up-to-date clinical knowledge and not having a great deal of time to read about the newest theories and findings. There are some useful compendiums that clinicians may find helpful when working with their most difficult-to-treat patients whether they are working with groups, families, or in individual sessions. Williams and Ell (1998) have compiled a number of easy-to-read and highly informational chapters on the latest research on mental health treatment. There are also a number of excellent textbooks that provide the latest updates on mental health research and they include Barlow and Durand (1999) and Nietzel, Speltz, McCauley and Bernstein (1998). It is more difficult to find guidance in the literature about working in groups with people who have schizophrenia. Notable articles and volumes on group treatment of schizophrenia include those written by Albert (1994) Bond and De Graaf-Kaser, (1990), Kanas (1996), Kates and Rockland (1994), Miller and Mason (1998; 1999), Nightingale and McQueeney, (1996), Tomasulo (1995), and Yalom (1983). The discussion of groupwork with schizophrenia in this article is based on the findings and clinical data in these and other publications as well as the author's experiences with patients. Clinical vignettes are provided to help illustrate suggestions for practice.

Working with positive, negative and disorganisation symptoms

When group members are asked to talk about their symptoms, it becomes clear that the course of the disease varies for each person. Andreasen et al. (1995) recognise the need for different treatment strategies for each of the symptom types, positive, negative and disorganisation. Clinicians who work with patients who have schizophrenia have long understood that group therapy is well poised to render symptom-specific treatment. To participate in group it is necessary for members to be at a level where they have some insight about being ill and this happens when their acute symptoms have at least partly remitted. All patients with this illness do not have to be at the same level of healing but they do need the ability to remain in the group for the session, usually between 30 and 50 minutes, to listen when others speak, and be able to communicate coherently. The number of sessions varies with each individual and the norms of each clinical setting; there are no rules and many patients stay in group for several years.

Group leaders may begin their work by asking patients about their symptoms and their ways of coping. Once group members feel safe and comfortable, they tend to share ideas about how they feel when symptoms appear and what works best for reducing symptoms and the related anxieties. Discussions ensue and members are likely to offer suggestions to others with similar symptoms. Strategies for working on the different types of symptoms become part of the group content.

Groups provide much needed work in reality testing for patients who experience hallucinations and delusions. Exercises such as role-playing, doubling and mirroring help group members test the extent to which their feelings make sense to the rest of the group. Group feedback addresses the reality of delusional material in a way that carries a low level of threat because it comes from peers who understand the disease.

Groups give negative symptoms patients support and encouragement for accomplishing tasks and planning for leisure time. For negative symptoms, weekly routines include having member to member discussions about weekend plans and then group collaboration in designing activities. The highly disorganised patients benefit from the structure and routines that groups offer.

Groups are also helpful for coping with and overcoming cognitive deficits that most patients experience, a condition directly related to schizophrenia. Exercises that include reading, listening and understanding can be made part of a group's daily routine and thereby help reduce the stigma associated with cognitive loss. Group members build mastery skills and self-esteem by helping each other. The group's sense of mastery is enhanced and fears decrease when members feel that they are able to help others (Miller & Mason, 1998).

All of this may be accomplished while the clinician keeps the group on a low level of expressed emotion, that is, a low level of criticism and anger. Research continues to support the idea that people who have schizophrenia function better when expressed emotion is kept on an even plane (Butzlaff & Hooley, 1998). Group members may express feelings of anger or fear, but emotional outbursts can be harmful and even induce a re-emergence of positive symptoms and disorganised speech. This in turn may frighten others in the group and cause an overall downturn in group effectiveness. Of course high levels of expressed emotion cannot always be prevented, but these exchanges should not be encouraged.

Group members may take what they have learned from their group experience to their life outside of the group. For example, if Sally fears going to a government office for her benefits because she gets confused and overwhelmed, Jim offers to accompany her. They both gain: Jim gets a sense of mastery that compensates for his loss of cognitive functioning and Sally gets help negotiating a difficult environment. Out-of-group activities require careful monitoring but they need not be discouraged. Clinicians who are concerned about intimacy among members should discuss sex and safe-sex practices with the group. As in all groups, it is important to bring out-of-group activities back to the group. Clinicians need to remain alert regarding out-of-group alliances keeping in mind that some may be beneficial. The benefits of decreased negative symptoms and isolation must be weighed carefully against the possibility of inappropriate or difficult to manage relationships.

Treating first episode and chronic patients separately.

The prevailing thinking today is that it is preferable to treat first episode patients separately and in groups that provide opportunities for peer-group experiences. The first episode of schizophrenia, defined as the first five years of the disease, is a crucial time when symptoms and functioning have the greatest effect on health and lifestyles (Lieberman, 1993). It is during these initial years that young people, mostly in their late teens and twenties, experience multiple relapses and hospitalisations. They may lose their jobs, drop out of school and give up contact with friends. The shame associated with 'losing one's mind,' the possible paranoid thoughts and newly acquired cognitive difficulties move them towards a state of self-inflicted isolation. There is also a significant stigma that is still associated with mental illness. All of these factors contribute to changing patients' lives, in a dramatic and profound way.

Miller and Mason (1998) emphasise the importance of having clinicians focus on the newness of the disease. At a time when patients are facing all the difficult developmental issues related to their age, they are also coping with having an incurable disease that robs them of their sense of reality and very poignantly their youth as well. Schizophrenia is an enormous burden on top of the typical concerns of young people: sex and sexuality, drugs, career options, relationships and independence from families. There is a feeling of solemnity that befalls these young people, one that is unmistakable to experienced clinicians.

Group session themes that the author has found to be helpful in working with first episode patients include: compliance with medication, psychoeducation, social skills training, group insight and cohesion, and alliances with other members and the leader. Discussions of sex, sexuality, pregnancy, sexually transmitted diseases and safe-sex strategies are additional important topics.

Perhaps the greatest fear of first episode patients is that they will become like the more chronic patients. It is not that they are unsympathetic; it is that they are afraid of getting tardive dyskinesia, looking disheveled and living an isolated lifestyle. The group becomes a place for expressing these fears and anxieties about future life chances. It also becomes a place for readjusting expectations and beginning the process of 'starting over.' Michael is an example of a first episode young man struggling to find himself and the way to re-build his life.

Michael is a 26 year-old, white male who had been assigned to a dangerous job in the army, working with explosives. When his symptoms got out of control (voices, extreme anxiety) he was discharged and he returned to live with his parents. After two hospitalisations he attends a day treatment program, and participates in a first-episode group.

I am trying so hard not to be sick, to be normal. I need time. I have no friends, no girlfriend. I can't handle it right now. I need to find out who I

*am and who I can be. I know I don't want to be sick forever and I don't want
to look like a sick person. I don't know if I will be but I don't want to be.*

Michael's fear of having schizophrenia is more likely to be
expressed among first episode peers than with chronic patients who
are more debilitated by the disease.

High functioning first episode patients may use groups for
emotional support and as a way to stay on-track with medication
regimens after they return to work or school. Group members may
want to take some time off to adjust to new time and travel schedules
but it is a good idea to allow them re-entry as needed. Clinicians
with groups that have a number of high functioning members may
find that evening hours are more practical for patients with jobs and
school commitments. For lower functioning members, it's a good
idea to encourage them to stay in the group for as long as possible
without taking leave of absence. They tend to need the consistent
structure that group provides. It is important that all first episode
patients understand that each person has his or her own rhythm
of healing, that relapses are always possible, and that the best way
to avoid a relapse is to stay in treatment and take medication as
prescribed. Again, this message is best communicated in group.

Participation in research

Many clinicians think it is unfair to recruit patients who have
schizophrenia for research studies. Their view is that these patients
may not fully understand the consent forms and the protocols.
Schizophrenia has drawn principal attention to this issue even
when studies show that people with other illnesses do not always
understand research protocols (Mason & Pollack, 1997).

However, the author's experience is that to the extent that any
non-scientist understands complicated medical protocols, patients
with schizophrenia are likely to be as capable as anyone when they
are not acutely psychotic. When there is psychosis, families can be
called upon to help determine if the patient would want to be in a
study. Suffering from schizophrenia should not make individuals

ineligible for potentially helpful new treatments. In the US, where it takes on the average 12 years for a newly developed drug to get to market, patients who enter studies have an edge in getting early treatment. Drug approval time may be shorter in Britain and Europe, but nonetheless, it is advantageous to get an early start on an effective new drug.

Once patients are in studies, groups can be used to give assurances and support to anxious patients and provide clinicians with a vehicle for monitoring compliance and health issues. Study-based groups have an enormous potential for furthering the safety aspects of research. The group leader helps alert the members to the signs of the onset of side effects and other health-related symptoms. A high rate of health problems in this population makes careful monitoring especially important. Patients with schizophrenia are often ill because they go for long periods of time without proper healthcare. Years of taking multiple medications and possibly substance abuse may also take their toll. However, the newly researched drug can bring about medical complications of its own. Weight gain is one example of a medical problem that is directly related to some of the new anti-psychotic medications. In groups, patients may discuss their feelings about gaining weight and offer suggestions to other members about weight control. At the same time the leader can keep a watchful eye on each research patient to report to medical staff untoward side effects or any sudden change in appearance or behaviour.

Groups are helpful for supporting patients who are frightened about getting side effects or become discouraged when there is no immediate progress. Anxieties related to participation in research are discussed and members offer support and encouragement to each other. Groups also help with patients' family problems related to taking part in the study. Family members may be ambivalent about research or they can be outright negative. When this happens, groups are especially helpful in supporting patients' independent decisions to participate.

Group leaders should to be well-trained clinicians with positive attitudes towards research. Their role calls for independence from family members, drug companies and principal investigators. They must understand the protocols, work well with the research staff and be willing to make unbiased recommendations including a recommendation that a patient should leave a study. Not every clinician is up to these tasks as is illustrated by the case of Jane.

Jane was the group leader for a mixed therapy group of three study patients and four non-study patients at a day treatment centre. When Peter, a study patient, experienced an increase in symptoms, Jane reported this to the study staff. Without waiting for the research staff to recommend action, she spoke with the client in a private session. She told him to consider his option to leave the study. Without actually suggesting that he leave, Jane may have influenced the client to make a decision based on her own feelings about the study. Later, when a researcher interviewed Jane, she stated that Peter was not right for the study and that she thought he was doing worse since he signed up, but researchers disagreed. The patient stayed in the study but this conflict was not good for Peter or for the group.

Jane's belief that Peter was doing worse in the study was legitimate. In her view it was her ethical duty to inform Peter of his right to leave, go back on standard medication and thereby avoid a possible relapse and hospitalisation. The researchers saw it differently. They were aware of a potential emergence of symptoms in the beginning stages of this new drug treatment. In addition, they knew that study patients and clinicians were often hyper-vigilant and readily attributed symptoms to new medications. The researchers believed that Jane erred in speaking to Peter before they conferred to make their recommendation. The researchers and Jane did not have an open line of communication before this event.

Discord between a group leader and researchers can have further negative consequences. In this illustration Jane's speaking with Peter may have sent a negative message about the study to the two other study participants in the group. Since group members often talk outside of group, Jane's discussion with Peter, reminding him of his option to leave the study, would be a likely topic for an out-of-group discussion. Even if it were not, group members are sensitive to subtleties, including the attitude of their leader toward a study. If they thought Jane were unfavourably inclined toward the research they too might adopt this attitude and consider their options to leave the study.

Working with racial and ethnic differences

Groups bring together patients from different racial and ethnic backgrounds. The culture from which members come may influence some of their delusions and may result in discriminatory statements. Group leaders need to listen with sensitivity to patients' delusional material even when it may include unfounded prejudices. While the leader should never agree with discriminatory statements, openly criticising clients for their views will ultimately result in losing patients' therapeutic alliances. Here is where the power of group helps out. Group members can usually be counted on to refute these statements and offenders are likely to be responsive to peers. Most schizophrenia group leaders develop their own style of managing prejudiced patients, but when there is a need for further guidance the literature is not especially helpful.

Researchers in schizophrenia have studied racial and ethnic differences in the course of this disease. In a comparison of Afro-Caribbean and White patients in the UK, the Afro-Caribbean patients experienced fewer negative symptoms and were subjected to longer hospital stays and involuntary admissions (Takei et al., 1998). When comparing British Afro-Caribbean and White patients with schizophrenia, another group of researchers found that second generation Afro-Caribbeans were more likely to have siblings with the disease (Hutchinson, et al., 1996). Therapists in the UK who treat Afro-Caribbean patients need to be sensitive to their patients' prior treatment experiences and watchful about their interactions with siblings. Groups can help facilitate an acknowledgment of these painful issues and can accelerate the process of letting go of hurtful and frightening memories. An additional consideration is that culture and ethnicity often affect patients' attitudes toward treatment. The case of Arthur illustrates this important point.

Arthur, a 22 year-old Japanese-American attending a day treatment program in the US consistently stated in group that he did not need to take his medications. He insisted that his family agreed with him and that they were urging him to stop treatment altogether. With his permission, the group leader invited his parents to meet with her in an individual session. Sure enough, they stated that Arthur did not need his medication and that he should return to work. The fact that they were both highly educated did not seem to have any effect. In their culture, mental illness was a humiliation, a shame to the family. Arthur had to hurry up and recover, and stopping neuroleptic medication was for them the first step in this process. Arthur did stop his medication, left group and went to work for his family. He did become more symptomatic but his family maintained him at home without further interventions from psychiatric professionals.

The group leader could not convince the family to cooperate with treatment even though she had several past experiences with Japanese-Americans. However, her knowledge of this culture did allow her to be more accepting of the treatment outcome. Japanese delusional content is likely to refer to being slandered and shamed while Europeans tend to focus on delusions of poisoning and religious themes of guilt and sin (Tateyama et al., 1998). Arthur's and his family's focus on the shame of having schizophrenia is understandable in light of typical Japanese culture.

Patients from all cultures often feel guilty about having a chronic illness and the burden it places on their families. Family members may be 'burnt out' after years of stressful accommodations to the difficulties and repeated disappointments. The group takes the role of the family and becomes the only place, the only hour in the week, where guilt is alleviated and there is a feeling of belonging. It is not uncommon to hear from patients: 'The group is everything to me,' 'I do not know where I would be without this group,' 'This is the only place where my feeling are important,' and the like. Anyone who has led these groups will recognise the familiarity of these statements.

Summary and conclusion

The treatment of schizophrenia, like that of other illnesses, requires careful updates of what we now know. Recent research findings and clinical experience have changed some of the ways experts in the field of schizophrenia approach treatment. Psychosocial interventions in conjunction with medication therapy are now viewed as the optimal treatment regimen. Group work is gaining in prominence in certain crucial treatment areas. Groups play important roles in:

1. working with the positive, negative and disorganisation symptoms;
2. creating specialised environments for patients in the first episode;
3. helping patients safely participate in clinical research; and
4. working on issues related to cultural diversity.

Research and clinical experience show that when groups are both supportive and educational they are most effective with this population. Groups are used to teach psychoeducational concepts, to do social skills training, to encourage peer support, and to aid in the monitoring of and coping with symptoms. In combination with medication therapy, groups give patients the opportunity to experience consistent care and makes it more likely that they will maintain a better quality of life.

The power of the group is irrefutable in helping patients re-establish their identity and achieve a dignified and productive place in society.

References

Albert, J. (1994) Rethinking difference: A cognitive therapy group for chronic mental patients. *Social Work with Groups*, 17, 105-121

American Psychiatric Association. (1994) *Diagnostic and Statistical Manual of Mental Disorders*. (4th ed.) APA: Washington, DC

Andreasen, N.C., Arndt, S., Alliger, R., Miller, D., and Flaum, M. (1995) Symptoms of schizophrenia, methods, meanings, and mechanisms. *Archives of General Psychiatry*, 52, 341-351

Barlow, D.H., and Durand, V. M. (1999) *Abnormal Psychology, An integrative approach*. Pacific Grove, CA: Brooks/Cole

Bond, G.R., and De Graaf-Kaser (1990) Group approaches for persons with severe mental illness: A typology. *Social Work with Groups*, 13, 21-36

Brabbins, C., Butler, J., and Bentall, R. (1996) Consent to neuroleptic medication for schizophrenia: Clinical, ethical and legal issues. *British*

Journal of Psychiatry, 168, 540-544

Butzlaff, R.L., and Hooley, J.M. (1998) Expressed emotion and psychiatric relapse: A meta-analysis. *Archives of General Psychiatry*, 55, 547-552

Edwards, J., Francy, S.M., McGorry, P.D., and Jackson, H.J. (1994) Early psychosis prevention and intervention: Evolution of a comprehensive community-based specialized service. *Behavior Change*, 11, 223-233

Essock, S.M. and Kontos, N. (1995) Implementing assertive community treatment teams. Psychiatric Services, 46, 679-683

Garland, J.A., Jones, H.E., and Kolodny, R.L. (1973) A model for stages of development in social work groups. in S. Bernstein (ed.) *Explorations in group work: Essays in theory and practice*. Boston: Milford House

Hutchinson, G., Takei, N., Fahy, T.A., Bhugra, D., Gilvarry, C., Moran, P., Mallett,R., Sham, P., Leff, J., and Murray, R.M. (1996) Morbid risk of schizophrenia in first-degree relatives of white and African-Caribbean patients with psychosis. *British Journal of Psychiatry*, 169, 776-780.

Hogarty, G.E., Kornblith, S.J., Greenwald, D., DiBarry, A.L., Cooley, S., Ulrich, R.F., Carter, M., and Flesher, S. (1997) Three-year trial of personal therapy among schizophrenic patients living with or independent of family, I: Description of study and effects on relapse rates. *American Journal of Psychiatry*, 154, 11, 1504-1513

Kanas, N. (1996) *Group Therapy for Schizophrenic Patients*. Washington, DC: American Psychiatric Press

Kates, J., and Rockland, L.H. (1994) Supportive psychotherapy of the schizophrenic patient. *American Journal of Psychotherapy*, 48, 543-561

Kopelowicz, A. and Liberman, R.P. (1998) Psychosocial treatments for schizophrenia. in P.E. Nathan, and J.M. Gorman (eds.) *A Guide to Treatments that Work*. (pp.190-211) New York: Oxford U. Press

Lieberman, J.A. (1993) Prediction of outcome in first-episode schizophrenia. *Journal of Clinical Psychiatry*, 54, (suppl. 3), 13-17

Mason, S.E., and Pollack, D. (1997) Informed consent with older clients. *Law and Social Work*, 7, 143-157

Mason, S.E., Bermanzohn, P.C., and Siris, S.G. (1998) Clinical trials and tribulations: Implementation processes in schizophrenia research outcome. *Psychiatry*, 61, 288-301

Marder, S.R., Wirshing, W.C., Mintz, J., McKenzie, J., Johnston, K., Eckman, T.A., Lebell, M., Zimmerman, K., and Liberman, R.P. (1996) Two-year outcome of social skills training and group psychotherapy for outpatients with schizophrenia. *American Journal of Psychotherapy*, 153, 1585-1592

Miller, R., and Mason, S.E. (1998) Group work with first episode schizophrenia clients. *Social Work With Groups*, 21, 19-33

Miller, R., and Mason, S.E. (1999) Phase-specific psychosocial interventions for first episode schizophrenia. *Bulletin of the Menninger Clinic*, 63, 499-519

Munich, R.L. (1997) Contemporary treatment of schizophrenia. *Bulletin of the Menninger Clinic*, 61, 189-221

Nietzel, M.T., Speltz, M.L., McCauley, E.A., and Bernstein, D.A.. (1998) *Abnormal Psychology*. Boston: Allyn and Bacon

Nightingale, L.C., and McQueeney, D.A. (1996) Group therapy for schizophrenia: Combining and expanding the psychoeducational model with supportive psychotherapy. *International Journal of Group Psychotherapy*, 46, 517-533

Scott, J.E. and Dixon, L.B. (1995) Assertive community treatment and case management for schizophrenia. *Schizophrenia Bulletin*, 21, 657-668

Scott, M.J., and Stradling, S.G. (1998) *Brief Group Counselling*. Chichester, England: John Wiley

Takei, N., Persaud, R., Woodruff, P., Brockington, I., and Murray, R.M. (1998) First episodes of psychosis in Afro-Caribbean and White people. An 18-year follow-up population-based study. *The British Journal of Psychiatry*, 172, 147-153

Tateyama, M., Asai, M., Hashimoto, M., Bartels, M., and Kasper, S. (1998) Transcultural study of schizophrenic delusions. Tokyo versus Vienna and Tubingen (Germany) *Psychopathology*, 31, 59-68

Tomasulo, D. (1995) *The Healing Crowd: The interactive behavioral model for people with mental retardation and chronic psychiatric disabilities.* (Available from author, 723 N. Beers Street, Holmdel, NJ 07733)

Williams, J.B.W., and Ell, K. (1998) *Advances in Mental Health Research: Implications for practice.* Washington, DC: NASW Press

Yalom, I.D. (1983) *Inpatient Group Psychotherapy*. New York: Basic Books

This chapter was first published in 2000 in *Groupwork* Vol. 12(2), pp.27-44

At the time of writing Susan E. Mason was Associate Professor of Social Work, Wurzweiler School of Social Work, Yeshiva University, New York

Multi-family group interventions with schizophrenia

Jane Hanvey Phillips[1] and Jacqueline Corcoran[2]

Summary: *The de-institutionalisation movement has increased the family care of individuals with schizophrenia. Models of Multi-family group intervention have developed to improve family members' knowledge about schizophrenia, to help families with their grief, loss, and other adjustment problems, as well as to improve their coping with a family member suffering from schizophrenia. By working with the families, multi-family interventions also hope to delay relapse of symptoms, improve medication compliance, and help the individual suffering from schizophrenia to gain vocational aptitude. This article reviews these outcomes from the empirical studies on multi-family interventions. Implications for clinical research and practice are discussed.*

Key words: *family care; relapse; medication compliance*

Schizophrenia is a disorder characterised by 'delusions, hallucinations, disordered speech, grossly disorganised or catatonic behaviour, and/or negative symptoms' (American Psychiatric Association [APA], 1994, p. 285). Positive symptoms are those that represent distortions or excesses of usual demeanour, such as delusions or hallucinations (APA, 1994; Farmer et al., 1998; Leff, 1996), whereas negative symptoms refer to impaired normal functioning, such as withdrawal, apathy, or diminished social interactions.

Annual prevalence rates of the disorder are based on the number of cases under treatment, or the number of new cases during a given time frame (Norquist et al., 1996). According to World Health Organisation (2000) statistics, this translates to approximately 45 million individuals worldwide suffering from schizophrenia.

In recent years there has been a trend to deinstitutionalise psychiatric patients and as a result family members are becoming increasingly affected by the illness as they attempt to care for their ill relatives (Leff, 1996). Individuals suffering from schizophrenia characteristically experience confusion and distortion of reality which in turn may contribute to a variety of consequences in the home: non-schizophrenic family members and an identified patient may engage in interactions that are emotionally problematic (Leff, 1996; Leff et al., 1989; Nugter et al., 1997), the illness may be denied or there may be unrealistic expectations of the patient (Randolph et al., 1994); or family members may feel anxious and vulnerable about living with a relative suffering from this condition (Anderson et al., 1986).

No specific 'cause' for schizophrenia has been identified and research shows that the antecedents of schizophrenia are complex. In a review of the research, Liberman (1986) suggests that a variety of nonspecific stressors, such as difficulties with employment, or tension in the household interact with psychobiological responses, including increased psychotic symptoms or depression, in contributing to the etiology of the disorder. The patient's family may contribute to stress, but may serve as a means of support as well. Therefore family intervention may benefit the patient as well as family members. Historically, researchers targeted family communication patterns as a cause of schizophrenia, and expected a cure to come about through changes in these patterns. Bateson, Jackson, Haley, and Weakland (1956) suggested that people with schizophrenia often found themselves in double bind situations. The double bind is a situation where the person caught up in it loses out whichever way the person responds. The double bind stems form sending two messages simultaneously: one directs the person to do one thing and the other directs that person to do the opposite. Often, one of these messages is communicated by words and the other through non-verbal cues. It was thought that if family members began to communicate clearly and directly with the individual, rather than using double binds, schizophrenia might be alleviated. However, the double bind hypothesis was not confirmed in subsequent research.

During the same years The concept of 'expressed emotion' was explored by Brown and his colleagues (1962) when they studied the relapse rates of recently released patients with schizophrenia. A positive relationship between a particular form of emotional involvement with the family and relapse was found, and it was then that the concept of expressed emotion emerged as a description of the home environment. Low expressed emotion households reflecting low levels of emotional involvement between family members; defined by an absence of hostility and overcontrolling behaviours. High expressed emotion households were those in which family members or the identified patient displayed hostility towards others, or attempted to dominate other family members (Brown et al., 1962).

Nowadays, the focus of intervention is on developing coping strategies for family members, finding ways to decrease tension in the home, controlling symptoms through the patient's compliance with medication regimes, and preventing relapse, without the expectation of a cure. Some of the major uses of groupwork in this area were reviewed by Manor (1999).

Working with the families

Two general approaches to interventions with schizophrenia can be noted. Several families may be involved in a psychoeducation or support group, or a single family may participate in family therapy. The focus of the present review is on multi-family group interventions in which several families participate in a therapeutic group. (For single-family interventions, the interested reader is referred to Corcoran and Phillips (2000). The approaches to multi-family interventions may be classified as either psychoeducational (Abramowitz & Coursey, 1989; Anderson et al., 1986; Cañive et al, 1993, 1996; Hugen, 1993; McFarlane, Link et al., 1995; McFarlane, Lukens et al., 1995; Posner et al., 1992; Reilly et al., 1988; Smith & Birchwood, 1987; Solomon et al., 1996; Solomon et al., 1997) or supportive (Kane et al., 1990) in their focus. It is likely that some groups adopt both approaches.

Psychoeducation groups range in length from a one-day, two-hour workshop (Reilly et al., 1988) to bi-weekly sessions for two years (McFarlane, Lukens et al., 1995; McFarlane, Link et al., 1995) with most groups run for six- to ten-week sessions (Cañive et al, 1993, 1996; Posner et al., 1992, Solomon et al., 1996, 1997). A key component of family psychoeducation is imparting information about the illness to family members so that they have realistic expectations for the patient (Anderson et al., 1986). Several key themes are included in psychoeducational interventions. One theme is the biological basis for the relative's illness; the patient is not responsible for the occurrence of the illness. Further, the patient does not control the illness and, therefore, is not being lazy or purposefully disagreeable when psychotic. Third, family members may alleviate some of the patient's distress by decreasing expectations of participation in the life of the family. Fourth, the struggles family members face are not unique to their family alone. Another theme is that theories about schizophrenia and its treatment are developed regularly; consequently, family members should retain a sense of hope.

In addition to providing information about the expected course of the illness, Anderson et al. (1986) have developed a psychoeducational intervention that also addresses the family's emotional responses to schizophrenia, which may include guilt, embarrassment, anger, or a variety of other emotions as well as a consideration of family strengths. An example of a family strength might be that the parents of the patient are mutually supportive and regularly provide each other with time away from home to allow a respite from the duties of caregiving.

Support groups characteristically utilise self-help strategies while promoting reciprocal interaction, self-disclosure and encouragement for members of the group (Kane et al., 1990). Discussions tend to be unstructured and relate to experiences of coping with a family member who suffer from schizophrenia. To date, few studies have evaluated the effectiveness of support groups in reducing caregiver distress among family members of individuals suffering from schizophrenia though there is some evidence that psychoeducational groups with support components have been able to increase coping abilities among their members (Kane et al., 1990). As evidence of the dearth of research on support-only groups, Kane's study of a short-term support group (two hours per week for four weeks) is the sole study which met inclusion criteria for the present review.

Whether the group is based primarily on providing of mutual support or also includes psychoeducation, the group modality in itself may provide many of the benefits of the intervention. The group may relieve burden and stress, leading to improved coping mechanisms for family members. In the group, members may disseminate information about resources and share experiences about the relative usefulness of resources. These support functions may serve to help families cope with the chronicity of the illness, especially by way of reducing stigma, normalising communications, and sharing parenting skills and suggestions with other group members (McFarlane, Link et al., 1995).

Research on the potential benefits of these groups have focused attention on gains both to the family member and to the individual suffering from schizophrenia. Groupwork with families has produced positive outcomes for the person suffering from schizophrenia as well as positive outcomes for other family members. A discussion of therapeutic outcomes for individuals suffering from schizophrenia will be addressed below and will be followed by a discussion of outcomes for family members. Before that, brief comments about the studies selected for this review will be made.

Selecting the papers for this review

Interest in the field of family intervention with schizophrenia has increased since the 1980s. Dixon and Lehman (1995), Gingerich and Bellack (1996), and Lam (1991) have written comprehensive reviews of previous research, and the studies which were published 1985 or later are also included in the present review. The present review is concerned only with more recent studies and addresses those published during 1985 or later. Only studies which report empirical data, those published in refereed journals, and those listed in the relevant computerised database are included. All of the studies are outcome-oriented. Six of the ten research studies included in the review employed experimental design with random assignment to conditions (McFarlane, Link et al., 1995; McFarlane, Lukens et al., 1995; Posner et al., 1992; Schooler et al., 1997; Smith & Birchwood, 1987; Solomon et al., 1996, 1997). Three of the studies employed quasi-experimental designs (Abramowitz & Coursey, 1989; Kane et al., 1990; Reilly et al., 1988). The other studies (Cañive et al., 1996; Hugen, 1993) may be considered pre-experimental designs due to the absence of control or comparison groups. In keeping with the emphasis of previous reviews, the present focus will be on interventions involving parents or other family members rather than those treatments designed solely for the person with schizophrenia.

Outcomes for the person suffering from schizophrenia

Outcome measures relative to the patient with schizophrenia have included relapse and rehospitalisation rates, medication compliance, and work-related activities. Findings in these areas will be summarised below.

Relapse rates

Relapse rates have been measured in a variety of ways in several studies to determine the efficacy of family group interventions. Rehospitalisation has been a common measure of relapse (Hugen, 1993; Posner et al., 1992; Reilley et al., 1988; Schooler et al., 1997). Relapse has also been defined as changes in symptomatology and social functioning as reported by significant others (Hugen, 1993) and 'the re-emergence of major psychotic, schizophrenic symptoms that had persisted continuously for a minimum of 7 days ...' (McFarlane, Link et al., 1995, p. 135).

In that four-year longitudinal study, McFarlane, Link et al. (1995) attempted to identify the characteristics of an intervention that produced the greatest benefits for patients and their families. They randomly assigned families to one of three treatment conditions: psychoeducational multi-family groups, single-family psychoeducation interventions, or family dynamic multi-family group interventions without a psychoeducational component. When considering relapse rates for highly symptomatic patients, they found that psychoeducational multi-family group interventions resulted in lower relapse rates than single-family therapy or the family dynamic multi-family group (McFarlane, Link et al., 1995; McFarlane, Lukens et al., 1995). During two years period, the psychoeducational multi-family group experienced significantly fewer relapse episodes.

In fact, by the end of four years, 78 percent of single-family intervention patients had experienced at least one relapse, whereas the multi-family intervention group had a relapse rate of only 50 percent. These findings were attributed to the extended social networks provided by the multiple-family group format which tended to absorb the distress found to accompany a psychotic episodes. The plausibility of this finding is borne out by the observation that when the same level of symptoms were present in families participating in single family interventions, the tension in the family escalated beyond that which could be mitigated by the therapist and family alone.

Comparable results were found by Hugen (1993) in a study on the effect of a one-day educational workshop provided for family members of patients hospitalised with schizophrenia. According to Hugen (1993), a significant number of family members reported reduced conflict in the home following treatment. Additionally, a significant number also reported lower rates of hospitalisation for the patient during the three months following the intervention than the three months prior to the intervention.

Caution must be exercised when interpreting hospitalisation as a measure of an intervention's success. Hugen (1993) suggests that 'hospitalisation is to some degree a function of family coping abilities and is used frequently as a supportive respite for family members themselves' (p.149). Another factor which bears consideration in some countries, most notably in the United States, is that inpatient hospitalisation may pose a financial hardship for many families. If neither public health care nor private insurance is available, a patient whose symptoms warrant hospitalisation may, due to financial constraints, remain unhospitalised. Thus, household affluence may be a predictor of hospitalisation rates.

Even with this caveat, it appears that relapse may be delayed or reduced as a result of including psychoeducation in the patient's therapeutic plan.

Medication compliance

The establishment and maintenance of a therapeutically effective level of medication is one of the most significant factors in reducing schizophrenic symtomatology. Once an optimal dose and schedule has been determined, compliance with the medication regime is considered essential for improvement in the symptoms of schizophrenia (Anderson et al., 1986; Falloon et al., 1985; Glick et al., 1991; Haas et al., 1988; Hogarty et al., 1991; Leff et al., 1989; McFarlane, Link et al., 1995; McFarlane, Lukens et al., 1995; Randolph et al., 1994; Schooler et al., 1997).

According to Schooler et al. (1997), medication dosage was related to relapse, with those patients who achieved optimal dosages being less likely to suffer relapse. McFarlane, Lukens et al. (1995) found that the rate of medication compliance was the highest in a multi-family psychoeducation group condition when compared with two other treatment conditions: a family-dynamics only group condition and a single-family intervention condition. Though not the sole measure of the effectiveness of an intervention, medication compliance is nonetheless a critical component in relapse prevention and remission. Psychoeducational family groups may facilitate better medication compliance and therefore promote successful therapeutic outcomes (McFarlane, Link et al., 1995).

Work-related activities

It may be difficult for people with schizophrenia to seek or maintain employment (Anderson et al., 1986). As a result of the disorganised thought processes common in schizophrenia, problems may include difficulty in communication or in fulfilling job obligations. The goal of vocational rehabilitation therapy, then, is to help the individual successfully navigate the job market. It is important that the individual has a work environment that is stimulating though not overwhelming. Employment situations may be greatly improved as the patient learns such coping skills as conflict resolution and the importance of personal hygiene, qualities which family members may successfully influence (Anderson et al., 1986).

Underscoring the importance of work-related activities as measures of family intervention efficacy, McFarlane, Link et al., 1995, and McFarlane, Lukens et al., 1995) conducted a two-year study of multi-family group and single-family group interventions in which they addressed employment issues. They found that patients whose families participated in group psychoeducation fared much better in terms of work-related activities than those patients whose families were involved in individual family psychoeducation. It is important to note that in this study, the identified patient was absent from family intervention sessions; thus a patient's improvement was seen to be a result of improvement in family functioning.

Outcomes for the families

Several researchers have focused on treatment outcomes for family members as well as the identified patient (Abramowitz & Coursey, 1989; Cañive et al., 1993, 1996; Hugen, 1993; Kane et al., 1990; Posner et al., 1992; Smith & Birchwood, 1987; Solomon et al., 1996, 1997). According to Anderson et al. (1986), the illness often has a catastrophic impact on family members. Therefore, therapeutic goals are not limited to improvement in patient functioning, but also include improvement in family functioning. Family outcome measures have focused on an increased knowledge of schizophrenia, understanding the meaning of expressed emotion constructs, coping behaviours and subjective distress or burden, depression, grief, and self-efficacy.

Knowledge acquisition

The dissemination of information about the illness is an integral component of interventions with people suffering from schizophrenia and their families. Posner et al. (1992) emphasise the need for families to learn about the antecedents and etiology of schizophrenia, issues related to medication and side effects, the effects of stress on exacerbating the patient's symptoms and the availability of community resources. A key variable, then, is the ability on the part of the patient and family members to learn and retain this information.

It is likely that participants in family psychoeducational groups will demonstrate immediate, though perhaps temporary, gains in their knowledge of schizophrenia. Cañive et al. (1993, 1996) in their studies of psychoeducational support groups in Spain found that patients' parents attained significantly higher scores on knowledge acquisition tests immediately following a six-week psychoeducation course than they did prior to the intervention. A follow-up study nine months later, however, revealed less knowledge of schizophrenia than immediately following the intervention, yet still significantly more than before treatment began. Similarly, Hugen (1993) reported knowledge retention for a period of three months following a one-day workshop for family members, while Smith and Birchwood (1987) reported similar findings with knowledge declining six months after treatment.

Other studies comparing psychoeducational groups with support-only groups have typically found little difference in knowledge acquisition (Kane et al., 1990) or even greater increases in knowledge about schizophrenia (Posner et al., 1992). In their study, Kane and her colleagues found that family members had spent a mean of six years adapting to life with a schizophrenic relative. The authors suggested that part of the coping process was the result of being educated by others who had found ways to cope in similar situations.

Expressed Emotion

Hugen (1993) and Smith and Birchwood (1987) conducted studies of multiple-family group interventions to determine their effectiveness in reducing expressed emotion or family conflict. Smith and Birchwood (1987) found that after a four week intervention, there were no differences between a family psychoeducational group and a comparison group (which was comprised of educational materials sent via the postal service), with both groups reporting reduced fear of safety after intervention. In a pretest/post-test study, Hugen (1993) found that, after three months, family conflict was greatly lessened subsequent to multi-family psychoeducational group intervention. It is likely that the psychoeducational materials presented in the Smith and Birchwood (1987) study served similar purposes for the experimental group and comparison group despite the different forms of dissemination (group presentation versus delivery by the postal system), and that this may account for the inability to discern differences between groups.

Coping behaviours and subjective distress or burden

For family members, the development of coping skills is essential to helping themselves and the patient. An important goal, therefore, in both psychoeducation and support group models of intervention, is that of providing management tools which aid family members in adapting to life with a chronically ill relative. In psychoeducational groups, relatives are reassured that caring for their own emotional and social needs is, in fact, beneficial to the patient; they are reminded that the caregiving relative is overwhelmed, with no external support, has fewer coping resources available to use while caring for the patient (Anderson et al., 1986).

Some families reside with patients with schizophrenia who may exhibit disorganised thinking and communication patterns, or engage in bizarre behaviour, though they probably do not pose a physical threat to anyone. Other families, however, find themselves in the difficult position of residing with a patient who engages in dangerous behaviours. These behaviours may be harmful not only to the patient but also to family members and may include threats of suicide, wandering away from home, violence against others, failure to use sound judgment, as well as anything that may cause harm or the threat of harm to oneself or others. In order to increase the level of safety in the home, it is important that strategies are in place to handle dangerous situations should they occur. During participation in group sessions, family members may benefit from learning about other families' plans to maintain safety and thereby devise their own safety plans as a way of coping with the threat of danger.

Coping skills have been a primary focus in research on family intervention (Abramowitz & Coursey, 1989; Cañive et al., 1993, 1996; Kane et al., 1990; Posner et al., 1992; Smith & Birchwood, 1987; Solomon et al, 1996, 1997). It is often expected that coping skills may improve during and after family intervention, and that an improvement in these skills may lead to better outcomes for patients and their relatives. Not surprisingly, it has been found that coping strategies were tied to a relative's level of distress about the illness, with the greatest distress leading to the least effective coping strategies. Correspondingly, the less able a relative was to employ coping strategies, the greater the distress (Kane et al., 1990). In one stream of research, it was also found that mothers suffered more subjective distress than fathers (Cañive et al. 1993, 1996); presumably because mothers were the primary caretaker for the patient.

Mixed findings have resulted from research on the effectiveness of psychoeducation in reducing burden. According to some studies, participation in psychoeducational groups did not produce changes in perceived burden or distress (Cañive et al., 1993, 1996; Posner et al., 1992; Solomon et al., 1996, 1997), while others reported reductions in the following areas: trait anxiety (Abramowitz & Coursey, 1989), fear of safety, and general stress (Smith & Birchwood, 1987). The length of treatment does not appear to account for the disparity in these findings, nor does the presence of the patient during group sessions. It must be noted, however, that burden has been described in many different ways. Further study will be necessary to determine whether multi-family psychoeducation groups contribute significantly to a reduction in stress and burden, or if perhaps other interventions may prove more effective.

Depression and grief

When considering variables related to burden and distress, depression and grief should be addressed. Depression is not an uncommon phenomenon in relatives of patients with schizophrenia (Anderson et al., 1986; Kane et al., 1990). Sadness and grief may result when a loved one fails to achieve expectations. Many hopes and dreams for the future may be shattered when family members realise the patient is unlikely to return to the level of functioning present before the onset of the illness. For parents whose only child has been diagnosed with schizophrenia, the sense of grief may be particularly intense. Spouses, as well, are likely to experience a sense of grief and loss after schizophrenia is diagnosed; they may mourn the loss of shared dreams for a future spent with a healthy companion (Anderson et al., 1986).

Kane et al. (1990) compared psychoeducational groups to support groups. They found that depression in the psychoeducation group decreased to a greater extent than in the support group. Clearly grief and depression have an impact on an individual's ability to function, thus further research in this area would be beneficial to determine the crucial aspects of an intervention in alleviating such symptoms. One suggestion, based on empirically validated research with other depressed populations, is to use cognitive-behavioural techniques for caregivers of schizophrenic members (e.g., Young et al. 1993) within psychoeducational group treatment. A cognitive-behavioural treatment method is compatible with psychoeducational assumptions, with its emphasis on learning of skills, problem management, and explicit description of treatment goals.

Self-efficacy

A family member's ability to understand the effects of mental illness on a relative and the ability to cope with these effects have been termed 'self-efficacy' (Solomon et al., 1996, 1997). Included in the concept would be such behaviours as refusing to accept blame for a relative's illness, encouraging other people to accept the ill relative, allowing the patient to provide as much care as possible for her/ himself, appropriately responding to psychotic behaviours, and utilising available resources to aid the family (Solomon et al., 1996).

Multi-family group psychoeducation deals very specifically with the elements of self-efficacy and these are the areas where the most positive outcomes have occurred. For example, Smith and Birchwood (1987), Solomon et al. (1996, 1997), and Hugen (1993), found significant improvements in self-efficacy, including more optimism about the family's role in the illness, and less self-blame following intervention.

Implications for future work

In light of the volume of research pertaining to family interventions in schizophrenia, several observations are relevant.

First, given the biological aspect of the disorder, family intervention in the absence of psychotropic drug treatment is not likely to be successful. A team approach to patient management, including medical intervention, is crucial to enhancing long-term positive outcomes.

Second, it is apparent that multiple-family group interventions provide a level of support not found in single-family interventions, regardless of the therapeutic modality employed, and that the support is a valuable resource for patients and family members. There may be additional factors operating in the group setting which provide protection against relapse, and are not present when treating individual families; notably the opportunities to create informal networks of mutual aid among members that operate outside the group sessions.

Third, multiple-family groups have the advantage of providing a cost-effective form of intervention for families dealing with schizophrenia. Due to the usually long-term nature of the illness, it behooves the mental health care provider and family to identify methods of therapy which will be financially accessible and feasible.

Fourth, most of the family interventions have included the mother as the primary caretaker of the individual suffering from schizophrenia, though caregiving is a shared role in many homes (Cañive, 1993, 1996). Although many researchers studied interventions that included married couples (Cañive et al., 1993, 1996; McFarlane, Link et al., 1995; McFarlane, Lukens et al., 1995; Schooler et al., 1997; Smith & Birchwood, 1987), the interventions were not specifically designed as marital therapy. In some cases it may be necessary to include marital therapy as a component of the intervention in that relationships between spouses, when one is a suffering from schizophrenia, are likely to be quite different from those between parents and children or other family members (Anderson et al., 1986).

Continued research is necessary to determine optimum treatment approaches for patients with schizophrenia and their families. Rigorous studies, using psychometrically sound measures, and widely-accepted design standards will facilitate the development of the most effective protocols. With the exception of research by Canive et al. (1993, 1996), Kane et al. (1990), and Posner et al. (1992), reliability and validity information for measurement instruments was frequently not reported, though in some cases (e.g., Solomon et al., 1996, 1997), this information was reported for most measures but was not always complete.

Finally, the current body of literature is disproportionately weighted toward the study of male patients, though the illness has been shown to affect females with equal frequency (APA, 1994). Additionally, though the disparity is not as great for ethnicity as it is for gender, many studies have employed samples that include a larger percentage of Caucasians than of other ethnic groups, leading to an inaccurate reflection of the distribution of schizophrenia in the population. Ideally, future empirical studies will address the varying needs of different groups of patients, including, but not being limited to: those who are married, those with dual diagnoses, those with substance abuse problems, the very young or very aged, and those who are resistant to treatment. In this way, important information will be understood about the responsiveness of various subtypes of people with schizophrenia to different multi-family components.

Meanwhile, it is encouraging to note that positive outcomes can result from family interventions for patients and families coping with schizophrenia. With adherence to a medication regimen and appropriate long-term family interventions, many individuals suffering from schizophrenia may hope to enjoy long periods of remission, with decreased severity of relapse and improved day-to-day functioning.

References

Abramowitz, I.A. and Coursey, R.D. (1989) Impact of an educational support group on family participants who take care of their schizophrenic relatives. *Journal of Consulting and Clinical Psychology*, 57, 232-236

American Psychiatric Association (1994) *Diagnostic and Statistical Manual of Mental Disorders* (4th ed.) Washington, DC: APA

Anderson, C.M., Reiss, D.J. and Hogarty, G.E. (1986) *Schizophrenia and the Family: A practitioners guide to psychoeducation and management*. New York: Guilford

Bateson, G., Jackson, D., Haley, J. and Weakland, J. (1956) Towards a theory of schizophrenia. *Behavioral Science*, 1, 252-256

Brown, G.W., Monck, E.M., Carstairs, G.M. and Wing, J.K. (1962) Influence of family life on the course of schizophrenic illness. *British Journal of Preventive Social Medicine*, 16, 55-68

Cañive, J.M., Sanz-Fuentenebro, J., Tuason, V.B., Vasquez, C. Schrader, R.M., Alberdi, J. and Fuentenebro, F. (1993) Psychoeducation in Spain. *Hospital and Community Psychiatry*, 44, 7, 679-681

Cañive, J.M., Sanz-Fuentenebro, J., Vasquez, C., Qualls, C., Fuentenebro, F., Perez, I.G. and Tuason, V.B. (1996) Family psychoeducational support groups in Spain: Parents' distress and burden at nine-month follow-up. *Annals of Clinical Psychiatry*, 8, 2, 71-79

Corcoran, J. and Phillips, J. H. (2000) Family treatment with schizophrenia. in J. Corcoran *Evidence-based Social Work Practice with Families: A lifespan approach*. (pp.428-501) New York: Springer

Dixon, L.B. and Lehman, A.F. (1995) Family interventions for schizophrenia. *Schizophrenia Bulletin*, 21, 4, 631-643

Farmer, R.L., Walsh, J. and Bentley, K.J. (1998) Schizophrenia. in B.A. Thyer and J.S. Wodarski (eds.) *Handbook of Empirical and Social Work Practice*: Vol. 1 (pp. 245-270) New York: Wiley

Falloon, I.R.H., Boyd, J.L., McGill, C.W., Williamson, M., Razani, J., Moss, H.B., Gilderman, A.M. and Simpson, G.M. (1985) Family management in the prevention of morbidity of schizophrenia: Clinical outcome of a two-year longitudinal study. *Archives of General Psychiatry*, 42, 887-896

Gingerich, S.L. and Bellack, A. S. (1996) Research-based family interventions for the treatment of schizophrenia. *Research on Social Work Practice*, 6, 122-126

Glick, I.D., Clarkin, J.F., Haas, G.L., Spencer, J.H. and Chen, C.L. (1991) A randomized clinical trial of inpatient family intervention: VI. Mediating variables and outcome. *Family Process*, 30, 85-99

Haas, G.L., Glick, I.D., Clarkin, J.F., Spencer, J.H., Lewis, A.B., Peyser, J., DeMane, N., Good-Ellis, M., Harris, E. and Lestelle, V. (1988) Inpatient family intervention: A randomized clinical trial: II. Results at hospital discharge. *Archives of General Psychiatry*, 45, 217-224

Hogarty, G.E., Anderson, C.M., Reiss, D.J., Kornblith, S.J., Greenwald, D.P., Javna, D. and Madonia, J.J. (1986) Family psychoeducation, social skills training, and maintenance chemotherapy in the aftercare treatment of schizophrenia: I. One-year effects of a controlled study of relapse and expressed emotion. *Archives of General Psychiatry*, 43, 633-642

Hogarty, G.E., Anderson, C.M., Reiss, D.J., Kornblith, S.J., Greenwald, D.P., Ulrich, R.F. and Carter, M. (1991) Family psychoeducation, social skills training, and maintenance chemotherapy in the aftercare treatment of schizophrenia: II. Two-year effects of a controlled study on relapse and adjustment. *Archives of General Psychiatry*, 48, 340-347

Hugen, B. (1993) The effectiveness of a psychoeducational support service to families of persons with a chronic mental illness. *Research on Social Work Practice*, 3, 2, 137-154

Kane, C.F., DiMartino, E. and Jimenez, M. (1990) A comparison of short-term psychoeducational and support groups for relatives coping with chronic schizophrenia. *Archives of Psychiatric Nursing*, 4, 6, 343-353

Lam, D.H. (1991) Psychosocial family intervention in schizophrenia: A review of empirical studies. *Psychological Medicine*, 21, 423-441

Leff, J. (1996) Working with families of schizophrenic patients: Effects on clinical and social outcomes. in M. Moscarelli, A. Rupp and N. Sartorius (eds.) *Handbook of Mental Health Economics and Health Policy*, Volume 1: Schizophrenia. (pp.95-101) Chichester: John Wiley

Leff, J., Berkowitz, R., Shavit, N., Strachan, Al, Glass, I. and Vaughn, C. (1989) A trial of family therapy v. a relatives group for schizophrenia. *British Journal of Psychiatry*, 154, 58-66

Liberman, R.P. (1986) Coping and competence as protective factors in the vulnerability-stress model of schizophrenia. in M.J. Goldstein, I. Hand and K. Hahlweg (eds.) (1986) *Treatment of Schizophrenia: Family assessment and intervention*. New York: Springer-Verlag.

Manor, O. (1999) Help as mutual aid: Groupwork in mental health. *Groupwork*, 11, 3, 30-49

McFarlane, W.R., Link, B., Dushay, R., Marchal, J. and Crilly, J. (1995) Psychoeducational multiple family groups: Four-year relapse outcome in schizophrenia. *Family Process*, 34, 127-144

McFarlane, W.R., Lukens, E., Link, B., Dushay, R., Deakins, S., Newmark, M., Dunne, E.J., Horen, B. and Toran, J. (1995) Multiple-family groups and psychoeducation in the treatment of schizophrenia. *Archives of General Psychiatry*, 52, 679-687

Norquist, G.S., Regier, D.A. and Rupp, A. (1996) Estimates of the cost of treating people with schizophrenia: Contributions of data from epidemiologic surveys. in M. Moscarelli, A. Rupp and N. Sartorius (eds.) *Handbook of Mental Health Economics and Health Policy*. Volume I: Schizophrenia (pp.95-101) Chichester: John Wiley

Nugter, A., Dingemans, P., Van der Does, J.W., Linszen, D. and Gersons, B. (1997) Family treatment, expressed emotion and relapse in recent onset schizophrenia. *Psychiatry Research*, 72, 23-31

Posner, C..M., Wilson, K.G., Kral, M.J., Lander, S. and McIlwraith, R.D. (1992) Family psychoeducational support groups in schizophrenia. *American Journal of Orthopsychiatry*, 62, 2, 206-218

Randolph, E.T., Eth, S., Glynn, S.M., Paz, G.G., Leong, G. B., Shaner, A.L., Strachan, A., VanVort, W., Escobar, J.I. and Liberman, R.P. (1994) Behavioural family management in schizophrenia: Outcome of a clinic-based intervention. *British Journal of Psychiatry*, 164, 501-506

Reilly, J.W., Rohrbaugh, M. and Lackner, J.M. (1988) A controlled evaluation of psychoeducation workshops for relatives of state hospital patients. *Journal of Marital and Family Therapy*, 14, 4, 429-432

Schooler, N.R., Keith, S.J., Severe, J.B., Matthews, S.M., Bellack, A.S., Glick, I.D., Hargreaves, W.A., Kane, J.M., Ninan, P.T., Allen, F., Jacobs, M., Lieberman, J.A., Mance, R., Simpson, G.M. and Woerner, M.G. (1997) Relapse and rehospitalization during maintenance treatment of schizophrenia. *Archives of General Psychiatry*, 54, 5, 453-463

Smith, J.V. and Birchwood, M.J. (1987) Specific and non-specific effects of educational intervention with families living with a schizophrenic relative. *British Journal of Psychiatry*, 150, 645-652

Solomon, P., Draine, J., Mannion, E. and Meisel, M. (1996) Impact of brief family psychoeducation on self-efficacy. *Schizophrenia Bulletin*, 22, 1, 41-50

Solomon, P., Draine, J., Mannion, E. and Meisel, M. (1997) Effectiveness of two models of brief family education: Retention of gains by family members of adults with serious mental illness. *American Journal of*

Orthopsychiatry, 67, 2, 177-186

World Health Organisation (1996) WHO information fact sheet N 130: Mental health. Retrieved June 11, 2000 from the World Wide Web: http://www.who.int/inf-fs/en/fact130.html

Young, J., Beck, A. and Weinberger, A. (1993) Depression. In D. Barlow (ed.), *Clinical Handbook of Psychological Disorders: A step-by-step treatment manual* (2nd ed.) (pp. 240-277) New York: Guilford Press

This chapter was first published in 2000 in *Groupwork* Vol. 12(2), pp.45-63

At the time of writing:
Jane Hanvey Phillips was a Doctoral Candidate, at the School of Social Work, University of Texas at Arlington
Jacqueline Corcoran was Assistant Professor at the School of Social Work, University of Texas at Arlington

Supporting voices
Groupwork with people
suffering from schizophrenia

Lynda Randall and Wendy Walker

This is an account of a group for schizophrenic people in an acute psychiatric unit attached to a general hospital. Workers in the unit had identified a number of (predominantly) young schizophrenic patients who were thought to be particularly vulnerable to suicide and who needed more help than had hitherto been provided in coming to terms with their illness. These patients possessed a good deal of insight into their condition and their symptoms were well controlled by medication, but they mourned the loss of previous life-styles and were saddened by their diminishing prospects. The authors describe the setting up of a task-centred, problem-solving group that also sought to develop and maintain communication skills; the choosing of an appropriate therapeutic approach; and the importance of multi-disciplinary communication in a hospital.
The group highlighted the feelings of loss and the need to regain control of their lives, experienced by people who are diagnosed as schizophrenic.

Key words: *acute ward; task-centred; problem-solving*

> The voices in my head hate my guts, they give me no rest and spurn all I love best. The voices tear my dreams apart and ravage my heart. They strangle every hope. The me in my head kills the child in me and the person that would be.

This brief self-description by a patient provides a graphic picture of what it feels like to be suffering from schizophrenia.

We work in a modern psychiatric unit attached to a large district general hospital. A substantial number of recently diagnosed schizophrenic patients pass through the unit. Most attention, time and help given to such patients had been on a one-to-one basis, usually by the doctors or nurses. The day hospital sometimes worked with a specific problem area, for example offering an anxiety management programme, social skills training or work experience. An informal 'drop-in' was also available for patients who wanted social contact rather than formal therapy. The social work department was involved in dealing with practical and emotional issues arising from the diagnosis of schizophrenia but again this was on an individual or family basis.

Whilst for some patients what was on offer was sufficient, there was concern in the multi-disciplinary teams that a number of patients needed more help in developing skills to cope with their illness if they were to have a reasonable quality of life. These patients had a good deal of insight into their condition and their symptoms were well controlled by medication, but they were fearful of deteriorating. They mourned the loss of their previous lifestyles and were saddened by their diminishing life prospects, for example in relation to employment, friendships and marriage. They often expressed suicidal ideas and a number of deaths by suicide in this group of patients encouraged our desire to provide more help.

We felt that groupwork would offer an effective method of helping such patients come to terms with and develop strategies for dealing with their illness. Literature and practice suggest that groupwork may offer a greater opportunity to share experiences, reduce feelings of isolation and enhance problem-solving skills than individual work is able to do.

Much has been written in recent years on working with the families of patients described as schizophrenic (Falloon and Pederson, 1985; Doane *et al.*, 1986; Tamer and Barrowclough, 1986). Such writings have helped to inform our own work. There was in the hospital a relatives' support group in which issues of family interaction were already being addressed. What we wanted to do (and what we felt this literature also encouraged us to think about) was to consider another important issue - the need for *patients* to develop their abilities to cope with their illness, the problems arising from it, and the role of stress in relation to the recurrence of schizophrenia.

The available literature on groupwork with schizophrenic patients can be somewhat disconcerting with its warnings about the dangers of insight oriented approaches perhaps provoking a psychotic episode; or alternatively under stimulating patients and thus encouraging apathy and withdrawal (Kanas, 1985). Informal discussions in the multi-disciplinary teams disclosed similar anxieties, and colleagues needed reassurance that we would not employ psychodynamic methods which used 'uncovering' techniques and excessive self-disclosure. We decided that group therapy using a task-centred, problem-solving approach which also maintained and developed communication skills would be of most value to our patient group. This approach has been shown to be useful with schizophrenic patients and some studies have shown this type of groupwork to be more effective in preventing relapse than medication coupled with individual work (Malm, 1982; Walker and Mcleod, 1982; Scott and Griffith, 1982).

After the informal discussions, we wrote up our ideas on the aims, objectives and composition of the group and our roles within it. The notes were circulated to the multi-disciplinary teams with an invitation to provide referrals. The criteria we established for group membership were that members should have been diagnosed as schizophrenic, that their symptoms were controlled by medication and that they should positively wish to join the group. We decided also on equal numbers of men and women, between six and eight of each. Because of the type of person being sought (insightful and with a relatively intact personality), members were likely to be in their twenties or thirties but we also considered people who had become schizophrenic in later life and who had had one or two recent episodes.

The purpose of the group was to provide support by recognising shared experiences, strengths and abilities which existed in spite of illness; to provide information and suggest strategies for coping with schizophrenia. (We likened the patients' position to the situation of a recently diagnosed person with diabetes being encouraged to work out how best to live with their illness.) It was intended that the group should also provide enjoyment and fun, and strengthen the members' orientation in the present by the use of games and communication exercises. We also hoped to explore the possibility of a self-help group growing out of the support group (as it came to be called).

We also gave the planning notes to prospective group members as we wanted to involve them in generating ideas for the group. Four issues in particular emerged in preliminary interviews with prospective members. First, most people felt they wanted the group membership to be 'closed' as soon as possible, perhaps after the first two meetings when a stable group had been established. It was felt that having a closed group would enable a trusting, friendly atmosphere to be established more readily. We also discussed the time-span of the group and the consensus seemed to be that 12 one hour meetings at weekly intervals would be sufficient and a manageable commitment for both staff and group members. Secondly, there was a strong demand for information about schizophrenia, its possible causes, treatment and outcome. Thirdly, as most people were anxious about being in a group, the idea of using games to break the ice was welcomed and, in fact, suggested spontaneously by some people who had been in groups before. Last but not least was the issue of confidentiality and feedback to the multi-disciplinary teams. It was agreed at the first group meeting that feedback could be given but that nothing would be disclosed without members' consent. Feedback was in two parts: first, a general report on the group, outlining subjects discussed so as to give some idea of what was important for this group of patients; and secondly, a short report about each individual, their experience in the group and what further assistance (if any) they wanted.

We have now run two groups involving 18 people and are planning to run similar groups on a regular basis in the unit. It seems helpful in reviewing our work to examine three separate but interdependent aspects of these groups: *co-working and planning, group processes* and *outcome*.

Co-working can be difficult as well as fruitful and we resolved to put a good deal of effort into learning how to work together in the pre-group planning stage. We chose to operate in this manner partly so as to provide a role model of co-operative interaction for all the group members. Early sessions were quite closely structured to help everyone to feel safe. However, after a couple of meetings this degree of structuring proved unnecessary -as we had hoped it would - and group members worked out how they wished to see the meetings structured. Figure 1 gives an example of the plan for

Figure 1

SUPPORT GROUP MEETING

TIME	WORKER	TASK	
5 mins	Lynda Randall Wendy Walker	**Introduction:** talk about last week's meeting; state the agenda for this week's meeting; introduce new members; give positive feedback for the hard work they engaged in last week.	
		Exercises	**Aims**
5 mins	Wendy	Name volley with softball	Remind people of names, introduce new people, relax people.
5 mins	Wendy	Name and action to identify self, to be copied by the whole group.	
5 mins	Lynda	Trust exercise – every member closes their eyes and names the person on their right and left, go round the circle twice.	Orientation exercise, make people aware of the here and now. Trust group.
40 mins	Lynda & Wendy	Group discussion of last week's brain storming and the ideas produced.	Prioritize areas they identify; encourage group to work together. Group cohesiveness.
5 mins	Wendy	Pass the squeeze.	Fun, group trust.

Feedback
All exercises went well, discussed relaxation exercise and it was agreed that those group members who wanted it, could stay and the rest could go for a coffee.

a meeting, typical of the outline of the first two meetings.

Our desire to structure the group was, we think, partly a measure of our own anxiety about the group process. How would group members interact? Would they interact at all?

In the first meeting we used a 'brainstorm' (a title greeted with some hilarity!) to generate ideas from members as to what they wanted from the group. This exercise generated sufficient material to plan subsequent meetings. The areas selected were information and discussion about schizophrenia; coping with friendships and making new friends; managing family relationships; and dealing with employment, unemployment and retraining for different, sometimes sheltered, work situations. There was an overall concern that the group would become a warm, caring setting within which members could talk openly and honestly about themselves. Group members felt isolated by their illness and wanted to talk about their experiences of schizophrenia with others who 'knew' their experience.

The groups became 'closed' after two meetings and it is interesting to look at the various reasons why people dropped out. Twelve people were invited to each group initially. Of the first group of six men and six women, one man left to return to his employment; and one woman decided after the first meeting that the group would be too 'intrusive' for her - she did not want to talk about herself or her illness. This view was shared by one of the men in the second group, which eventually continued with four men and four women. One man and one woman did not attend as they had returned to work. Another man left because, although interested in the group, he could not motivate himself sufficiently to attend - *7 know I'd enjoy it if I got there but I can't get out of bed in the morning'.*

The feedback after covering all the topics suggested made it clear that the most valued aspects of the group experience were the information gained about their illness, its origins, treatment and prognosis; and the opportunity to share with other sufferers their experiences of the illness and its impact on their lives. Joan*, for example, said:

> *I feel so guilty about the voices telling me to hurt the children. I know it's not me but it makes me feel bad ... it's such a struggle not to hear the voices. It helps me to know that other people have the same experience, that it's an illness and that it's possible to cope.*

Or Pat, who said:

> *If I meet someone who I think might be a friend, I always tell them I am schizophrenic - then I lose them - I feel I should be honest.*

To which Dave responded:

> *I establish a friendship and when I'm sure it's OK I might say I have a problem with my nerves but I don't say I'm a schizophrenic until I think they can*

take it - after all, when we're well we're the same as other people - there's
no need to look for trouble.

Some group members decided to set up a self-help group, which will help to fill an unmet need in the locality, providing a valuable community resource. We agreed to introduce a community worker who had expertise in facilitating self-help groups and we are now involved only as somewhat distant contacts for this group.

We conclude this paper with a few points which we feel it is important to bear in mind in groupwork with people described as schizophrenic. First, it is important to be sensitive to the amount of emotional disturbance which they may be able to tolerate. Some members, for example, were adamant that they would not talk about their families as this would be too upsetting. Some did not want to get too close to people as they felt too threatened, and we felt it was important to respect their wishes.

*names have been changed in the interests of confidentiality
In seeking to achieve an appropriate level of stimulation it is helpful to use physical exercises. Many schizophrenic patients are 'slowed down' emotionally and physically and a variety of activities can release latent energy and relax tensions.

It is also necessary to consider how to manage difficulties which may arise from two particular symptoms of schizophrenia, thought disorder and flattening of affect. In relation to thought disorder, some members found it difficult to concentrate and would apparently wander off the subject under discussion. One example was Andrew, a very withdrawn young man, who commented in several meetings:

> My uncle wants me to buy a house. I've been living out in the field next door
> to him and now he's going to buy me a house.

Attempts made to decode Andrew's comment (sometimes the only remark he made in the meeting) met with little success until the group decided to devote an entire meeting to housing and family problems. It then became clear that although Andrew's comment was based on a delusion - he was in fact living at home with his parents - he did need to find somewhere to live as his family home was overcrowded. It is probably significant that those who showed most signs of thought disorder did not become involved in the self-help group.

Flattening of affect was movingly described by Caroline, as follows:

> *I can remember the day when my feelings stopped. I know that I love my children but I cannot feel what that means any more. I have to go through the motions and it's an act. On a bad day I cannot do that: I am unresponsive, I cannot be happy or sad - just flat.*

Some people did not have her insight and were flat most of the time. This could be disconcerting. For example, if a group member disclosed something that upset them, some group members seemed offhand and uninterested, which was hurtful. Caroline's comment touched people and enabled them to respond to others more sensitively.

It is important to appreciate the significance of the patient role. There is something about 'being a patient' that seems disabling from the point of view of coming to terms with and understanding illness. It was clear that although a fair amount of information had been given to group members by their doctors, it had not been absorbed. The passivity of the 'patient patient' who expects to be acted upon rather than being an actor inhibits the gaining of knowledge and therefore some control over the impact and meaning of the diagnosis of schizophrenia. Those who had been out of hospital for more than two months seemed more able to be 'actors' than those more recently discharged.

Finally, related to the wish for information, is the importance of repetition and sharing of experience and knowledge in coming to terms with their illness. All the group members wanted to recapitulate their experience of illness in a way that seemed to be an attempt to own their illness and thus themselves. Before joining the group, they had tended to see themselves as having 'split' personalities, a healthy self and a sick self that is 'out there' and dependent on others for its care - this perception of being split reflecting the popular view of schizophrenia. Being in the group - with its supporting voices - seemed to enable members to begin to heal the split in themselves, both emotionally and cognitively.

References

Doane, J.A., Goldstein, M.J., Miklowitz, D.J. and Falloon, I.R.H. (1986) The impact of individual and family treatment on the affective climate of families of schizophrenics. *British Journal of Psychiatry*, 148, .279-287

Falloon, I.R.H. and Pederson (1985) Family management in the prevention of morbidity of schizophrenia: the adjustment of the family. *British Journal of Psychiatry*, 147 156-163

Kanas, N. (1985) In-patient and out-patient group therapy for schizophrenic patients. *American Journal of Psychotherapy*, 39, 3, 431-439

Malm, U. (1982) The influence of group therapy on schizophrenia. *Acta Psychiatrica Scandinavica*, 65 (Supplement 297)

Scott, D. and Griffith, M. (1982) The evaluation of group therapy in the treatment of schizophrenia. *Small Group Behaviour*, 13, 3, 415-422

Tarrier, N. and Barrowclough, C. (1986)Providing information to relatives about schizophrenia: Some comments. *British Journal of Psychiatry*, 149, 458-463

Walker, J.l. and McLeod, G. (1982) Group therapy with schizophrenics. *Social Work*, 27, 4 364-367

This chapter was first published in 1988 in *Groupwork* Vol. 1(1), pp.60-61

At the time of writing:
Lynda Randall was a Social Worker in the Psychiatric Unit of Leicester General Hospital
Wendy Walker was an Occupation Therapist at Leicester General Hospital

Evaluative study of group work for stress and anxiety

Rhona Birrell Weisen

This paper describes a pilot study of the effectiveness of group work for stress and anxiety. The groups studied were based in community settings and were led by group leaders of different professional backgrounds. The groups were evaluated using the Beck Anxiety Inventory as a measure of anxiety symptomatology, and a 'ways of coping' questionnaire as a measure of coping strategies. The results of this study provide some evidence for the effectiveness of these groups in helping people to deal with anxiety, and suggest that the therapeutic value of these groups may be related to the reduction of maladaptive coping strategies.

Key words: *groupwork effectiveness; anxiety; Beck Anxiety Inventory*

Introduction

With the growing understanding of stress and anxiety, there has also been a growing interest in developing ways of dealing with these problems. To date, much of the evaluative research of the methods being developed has been concerned with stress management and anxiety management training for clinical patients in treatment programmes, usually with clinical psychologists and psychiatrists (Woodward and Jones, 1980; Jannoun et al., 1982; Barlow et al., 1984; Powell, 1987). However, there are also less formal groups in community settings, generally intended for people experiencing ill-effects of stress and anxiety, led by group leaders from different professional backgrounds. In the light of the lack of evaluative studies of these small and varied informal groups for non-clinical clients this study was carried out in order to gain an overall impression of the effectiveness of such groups as they are currently running.

Effectiveness was measured in terms of whether or not the groups were successful in reducing anxiety symptoms, in reducing maladaptive ways of coping and in promoting more adaptive ways of coping with stressful life experiences. When observing changes in anxiety symptomatology and psychological ways of coping with stress it is also interesting to examine the relationship between these changes (as is suggested in Snyder, 1984). The second intention of this study is therefore to determine whether or not reductions in anxiety symptoms bear any relationship to changes in ways of coping, in order to gain insight into the ways in which these groups are most effective.

The groups

Five groups for stress and anxiety management were included in this study (these were the only such groups, known to the researcher, to be running in the Oxfordshire area at the time of the study). The groups are similar in three important ways: they each include open group discussion of personal experiences of stress and anxiety, as well as focused discussion and activities that facilitate understanding of stress and anxiety. In addition they teach applied relaxation as an active coping skill, with particular emphasis on progressive muscular relaxation, breathing exercises, and the home practise of relaxation techniques. On the basis of these similarities the groups were taken together as 'groupwork for people with problems related to stress and anxiety'. There was no attempt to standardise the groups, since this study, as a pilot study, aims to get an overall impression of the effectiveness of the type of groups described here. However the groups do differ on a number of variables, posing significant limitations to the conclusions that can be drawn from this research. They were groups of different sizes and duration, with varied programmes of activities (which are briefly described below). Also, groups 1 and 2 have elements of anxiety and panic management using cognitive therapy techniques which are not used in the other groups.

Group 1

The setting	Cowley Community Centre
Group leader	psychology graduate
Co-leader	psychology graduate

A nine week course, one and a half hour session once per week; a closed group with eight members (of whom four completed the questionnaires). Each session was divided into three parts:

1. 15 minute general discussion;
2. a one hour discussion of the theme for the session (including facts about stress and anxiety, the role of relaxation, coping strategies, panic management);
3. 15 minutes of progressive physiological relaxation, breathing exercises (and relaxation using visual imagery in some sessions).

Group 2

The setting	Cowley Community Centre
Group leader	psychology graduate
Co-leader	clinical psychologist (weeks 4-8)

An eight week course, one and a half hour session once per week; a closed group with four members (all of whom completed the questionnaires). Each session was divided into three parts:

1. 15 minutes general discussion;
2. one hour's discussion on the theme for the session (including facts about stress and anxiety, recognising anxious thoughts, panic management, problem-solving and goal setting);
3. 15 minutes of progressive physiological relaxation, breathing exercises (and relaxation using visual imagery in some sessions).

Group 3

The setting   Thame Health Centre
Group leader   occupational therapist

A six week course, a two hour session once per week; a closed group with eight members (of whom four members completed the questionnaires); 17 people started the course, but nine dropped out before completing it. Each session was divided into three parts:

1. 10-15 minutes discussion of the theme being introduced in the session (including the role of relaxation in stress management, self awareness and assertiveness, problem-solving and goal setting):
2. one and a quarter hours of more general group discussion;
3. half an hour of progressive physiological relaxation, and breathing exercises.

Group 4

The setting   Witney Community Centre
Group leader   community psychiatric nurse

A six week course, one and a half hour session once per week; a closed group with five members (of whom three completed the questionnaires). Each session was divided into two parts:

1. discussion, including facts about stress, anxiety and relaxation;
2. progressive physiological relaxation, and relaxation using visual imagery.

The final three sessions included more general group discussion (including discussion of stresses related to family, work and social relationships).

Group 5

The setting	Bampton Castle Health Centre
Group leader	health visitor

A six week course, one hour session once per week; a closed group with ten members (of whom eight completed the questionnaires). Each session was divided into three parts:
1. 10-15 minutes general discussion;
2. 20 minutes discussion of the theme for the session (including facts about stress, the role of relaxation and massage as strategies for coping with stress);
3. 15-20 minutes of progressive physiological relaxation.

Method

Participants

The participants in this study were people who attended one of the five groups for stress and anxiety. Only people that had attended a minimum of four sessions of their respective course (including the final session), and completed all of the questionnaires, were included in the study (*n*=23, 18 females and 5 males; from a total of 35 people who completed the first set of questionnaires).

The control group were members of Acorn, a voluntary sector day centre 'drop-in' for people with mental health problems. All members of the centre were asked to complete the questionnaires. However only those people who completed all of the questionnaires, and who scored above 10 on the first Beck Anxiety Inventory, were included in the control group (*n*=16, 6 females and 10 males: from a total of 33 people who completed the first set of questionnaires). The cut-off point of a score of 10 on the Beck Anxiety Inventory (BAI) was chosen to ensure that people in the control group had similar initial BAI scores to the participants in the study groups.

The study group and 'no-group' control were only matched in terms of their scores on the BAI.

Questionnaires

The Beck Anxiety Inventory (Beck, 1970) is a self-report measure of anxiety symptomatology. Common anxiety symptoms are listed (including 'rapid breathing', 'heart pounding', 'hands trembling') to which the participant responds by indicating how severely each symptom has been experienced in the previous week: not at all, mildly, moderately or severely. The BA! was used in this study in order to compare the experience of anxiety symptoms before and after participation in the groups for stress and anxiety.

A shortened version of the Lazarus and Folkman (1984) 'ways of coping' questionnaire (see appendix) was used in this study to compare the use of adaptive and maladaptive ways of coping before and after participation in the groups for stress and anxiety. 'Ways of coping' are determined in terms of how the person reports that he or she has reacted to recent anxiety-provoking situations; these responses are weighted from 0 to 3 depending on how often each was used: whether not used, used somewhat, quite a bit or a great deal. The original questionnaire was reduced from 59 to 24 items in order to limit the time spent on completing the questionnaires and to avoid excessive disruption of the groups. Items were selected that were particularly clear and which should need little or no explanation by the group leader. Also the items were selected to cover key ways of coping that are particularly relevant in groupwork for stress and anxiety, including ways of coping which are often encouraged as well as those which are discouraged. For the purposes of this study, ways of coping which are usually encouraged were counted as adaptive coping strategies (of which there were 18 items). These included reactions such as: looking on the bright side of things, letting one's feelings out, seeking advice, making an effort to understand and resolve the situation. Ways of coping which are discouraged were counted as maladaptive coping strategies (of which there were 6 items). These included reactions such as: drinking alcohol or using drugs, keeping the problem to oneself, criticising or lecturing oneself. It is conceivable that, for example, 'looking on the bright side' could be a maladaptive way of coping if it encouraged avoidance of a problem that exists. On the other hand, 'keeping the problem to oneself could in some cases be an adaptive way of coping. It is clear that the definition and measurement of adaptive and maladaptive ways of coping is debatable, and is an area which in itself merits further study.

Procedure

Groups for people with problems related to stress and anxiety were located in the Oxfordshire area. The group leaders were contacted and all agreed to take part in the evaluative research. All group leaders were given clear instructions, both verbally and written, as to how to administer the questionnaires. They were asked to give out the Beck Anxiety Inventory at the beginning of the first session of their next course. The 'ways of coping' questionnaire was to be completed at the beginning of the second session. In the final session both questionnaires were to be given out once more. When administering the questionnaires the group leaders were instructed to tell subjects that these were to be completed as part of a study of groupwork.

The control group completed the BA! and the 'ways of coping' questionnaire at the beginning and end of a six to eight weeks period

Results

Table 1
Means and standard deviations for study group and control on the BAI and ways of coping scores, pre-group and post-group.

Variable		Study group (N=23)		Control (N=16)	
		Mean	SD	Mean	SD
BAI	Pre-group	22.44	12.94	26.25	13.19
	Post-group	12.91	8.06	22.44	11.30
Adaptive coping	Pre-group	19.70	6.56	15.81	4.04
	Post-group	20.44	8.02	14.25	5.94
Maladaptive coping	Pre-group	9.52	3.36	9.37	3.81
	Post-group	6.17	3.46	8.44	4.15

Pre-group and post-group BAI and ways of coping scores were examined to test for statistical differences between the study group and control at the beginning and end of the study. Due to a skewed frequency distribution non-parametric statistics were applied, namely the Mann-Whitney test. This statistic tests for the significance of differences between the distribution of scores, as opposed to differences between mean scores. However, the results of the Mann-Whitney tests do reflect the trends shown for the mean scores (Table 1).

The significance of differences between the study group and the control on pre-group measures was determined using two-tailed tests, since no differences were predicted. Predicted differences on post-group measures were examined using one-tailed tests. It was expected that participation in a group for stress and anxiety should result in a reduction in anxiety symptoms, as well as an increase in adaptive ways of coping and decrease in maladaptive ways of coping.

Results for Beck Anxiety inventory scores

The initial, pre-group scores on the BA! were not significantly different for the study group and control. At the end of the study, post-group scores were significantly less for the study group than for the control ($Z=2.63$, $p=O.004$). This suggests that there was a significant reduction in anxiety symptoms for the participants in the groups for stress and anxiety.

Results for adaptive ways of coping

Pre-group scores on adaptive ways of coping are significantly different for the study group and control ($Z=2.17$, $p=O.03$). Post-group scores are also significantly different ($Z=2.24$, $p=O.01$) and although more significant this result does not offer a useful basis for determining the effect of participation in the study group in view of the initial, pre-group differences between the study group and control. In this case perhaps the mean pre-group and post-group scores are more informative (Table 1); it is apparent that there are no marked improvements in mean adaptive ways of coping scores for the study group or the control.

It may be worth noting that pre-group mean adaptive ways of coping scores are significantly higher for the study group, perhaps reflecting a difference between anxious people who join groups for stress and anxiety and those who do not. It seems plausible that making the decision to join a group presumes there is already a higher level of adaptive ways of coping.

Results for maladaptive ways of coping

The initial, pre-group maladaptive ways of coping scores were not significantly different for the study group and control. Post-group scores were significantly different (Z=1.64, p=O.048), showing a significant reduction in maladaptive ways of coping for the study group only.

Correlation between reductions in anxiety symptoms and changes in ways of coping scores

Further analysis of the results revealed that for the study group members there was a significant correlation between the reduction in maladaptive ways of coping scores and decreases in BAI scores (r=0.63, DF=22, p>O.05), indicating a positive relationship between reducing maladaptive coping strategies and alleviating anxiety symptoms.

Within group comparisons

When the groups within the study group sample were examined independently there were no significant differences found on pre-group and post-group scores. Also, when groups 1 and 2 (as groups including cognitive therapy techniques in anxiety and panic management) were compared to the other groups, no significant differences were found. It is very likely that the numbers in each group were too small and too varied to bring out any significant differences between the groups.

Initial BAI and ways of coping scores of people who dropped out of the groups for stress and anxiety were compared to the scores of the study group in order to determine whether there are any trends which may help to explain why some people dropped out of these groups. There were in fact no significant differences between the initial scores of dropouts and those who finished the groups. It is, however, noted that all the people who dropped out were from group 3, which started with 17 members; suggesting that this group size may be too large for effective groupwork for stress and anxiety.

Discussion

The pilot study described in this paper provides evidence that groupwork for stress and anxiety in community settings can be effective. There is at least an indication that these groups for non-clinical populations, led by group leaders of different professional backgrounds, are effective in alleviating anxiety and in improving strategies for coping with stress. Participants in the groups for stress and anxiety showed a reduction in anxiety symptoms that was greater than that of people in the control, who did not take part in any such group. Significant reductions in maladaptive ways of coping were noted for participants of the study groups, and also a significant correlation between decreases in the Beck Anxiety Inventory scores and decreases in maladaptive 'ways of coping' scores. There was no evidence of improvements in adaptive ways of coping. Tentative conclusions from these findings would suggest that changes in maladaptive ways of coping were more readily achieved by attendance at these groups than were changes in adaptive ways of coping, and that the therapeutic value of these groups could stem from helping people to reduce their maladaptive coping strategies.

The limitations of the design of this study should be taken into account when interpreting these conclusions; bearing in mind the differences between the groups studied as groupwork for stress and anxiety, the limitations of the measurement of adaptive and maladaptive coping strategies, and that the study group was only roughly matched to the control. In a future better controlled study, each person could act as his or her own control if anxiety levels and ways of coping could be measured some time before involvement in a group (which may be possible in groups that have a waiting list of people for a future course).

This study points to the need to investigate further the way in which coping strategies can be expected to be influenced by participation in groups for stress and anxiety. The results of this study suggest that it may be easiest to effect changes in maladaptive coping strategies.

It could be interesting to see if measures of adaptive and maladaptive ways of coping could help to screen for people most likely to benefit from groupwork for stress and anxiety. The higher initial adaptive ways of coping scores of the participants of the study group suggests that the measurement of adaptive ways of coping could be a potentially useful way of identifying which people are ready to make effective use of such groups. Further study of why people drop out of groups may also prove useful in determining whether readiness or suitability for group membership could be measured in terms of initial ways of coping scores.

The classification of adaptive and maladaptive coping strategies requires further study, and the measurement of adaptive and maladaptive coping strategies will need to be more carefully developed and tested if we wish to explore groups further in these ways.

Further research should explore which types of groups for stress and anxiety are most effective, in terms of factors such as the number and length of sessions, number of members, leadership style and group activities. Evaluation of groupwork in community settings for non-clinical clients will rely on the use of research methodologies that are compatible with the informal nature, flexible structures and varied programmes of these often small and independent groups.

Appendix

The following 24 items were selected from the Lazarus and Folkman questionnaire.

1. I tried to analyse the problem to understand it better.
2. Turned to work or substitute activity to take my mind off things.
3. Looked for a silver lining, so to speak; tried to look on the bright side of things.
4. I did something which I didn't think would work, but at least I was doing something.
5. Talked to someone to find out more about the situation.
6. Criticised or lectured myself.
7. I told myself things that helped me to feel better.
8. Kept others from knowing how bad things were.
9. Avoided being with people in general.
10. I made a plan of action and followed it.
11. I let my feelings out somehow.
12. Got away from it for a while; tried to rest or take a vacation.
13. Tried to make myself feel better by eating, drinking, smoking, using drugs or medication.
14. Rediscovered what is important in life.
15. I asked a relative or friend respected for advice.
16. Made light of the situation; refused to get too serious about things.
17. I prepared myself for the worst.
18. I knew what had to be done, so I doubled my efforts to make things work.
19. Came up with a couple of different solutions to the problem.
20. Accepted it, since nothing could be done.
21. I changed something about myself.
22. I daydreamed or imagined a better place than the one I was in.
23. I tried some physical exercises.
24. I tried something other than what is covered above.

Items 6,8,9,13, 17 and 20 were scored as maladaptive ways of coping. The remaining items were scored as adaptive ways of coping.

Acknowledgements

The author wishes to thank the group leaders for their patience in administering the questionnaires, and for their enthusiasm in support of this study.

References

Barlow, D.H, Cohen, A.S., Waddell, M.T., Vennilyea, B.B., Klosko, J.S., Blanchard, E.B., and DiNardo, P A. (1984) Panic and generalized anxiety disorders, nature and treatment'. *Behaviour Therapy,* 15, 431-449

Beck, A.T. (1970)*Anxiety: Causes and treatments.* University of Pennsylvania Press.

Jannoun, L., Oppenheimer, C., and Gelder, M. (1982) A self help treatment programme for anxiety state patients. Behaviour Therapy, 13, 103-111

Lazarus, R.S. and Folkman, S. (1984) *Stress, Appraisal and Coping.* New York: Springer

Powell, T.J. (1987) Anxiety management groups in clinical practice: A preliminary report. *Behavioural Psychotherapy,* 15, 181-187

Snyder, M. (1984) Progressive relaxation as a nursing intervention: An analysis. *Advances in Nursing Science,* April

Woodward, R. and Jones, R.B. (1980) Cognitive restructuring treatment, a controlled trial with anxious patients'. *Behaviour Research and Therapy,* 18, 401-407

This chapter was first published in 1991 in *Groupwork* Vol. 4(2), pp.152-162

At the time of writing, Rhona Birrell Weisen was with the Division of Mental Health, WHO, Geneva

'Cycling over Everest': Groupwork with depressed women

In England, there are fewer and fewer opportunities for social workers to undertake groupwork. The following is a description of an innovative feminist approach involved in adapting psychoanalytic theories, particularly the work of Winnicott, within a groupwork context. The paper describes a typical group session, preceded by an account of some of the main theories and practices informing our work.

Key words: *feminist approach; psychoanalytic theories; depression*

Womankind, a women and mental health project, was started in 1986 and is based in Bristol, England. Many of its founders were social workers and this professional link has remained a major influence on our work.[1] We have now been running depression groups for the past eight years and currently run three weekly groups where we are attempting to develop an approach to meet the needs of women whose history is of depression and disadvantage. This involves exploring whether psychodynamic theories and practices can be usefully adapted and applied, within a feminist framework, to help us to understand the impact of oppression and injustice on women's psychological development and what can be done in terms of practice, from both a personal and political standpoint, to prevent further oppression and to assist women to recover from the pain and defeats already experienced.

Our tentative journey toward psychodynamic theories and practices began with the realisation that a knowledge of women's oppression, and a passion for justice, were not enough. Women were raising issues in our groups at a level where our responses were beginning to feel superficial and unhelpful. For example, whilst it was clear that women gained a great deal from being with one another, the capacity of some women to remember and take in these and other positive experiences remained an ongoing problem. Despite the understanding that women were gaining about the ways that sexism had limited or distorted their experience of themselves and others, and the positive changes they had been able to make in their lives, for some women these changes felt hollow because they did little to alter their depression and their low feeling of self worth in relation to themselves and the future. We had to rethink our view that positive changes in the external world necessarily produced comparable changes in women's internal world: some of the same feelings of deprivation continued to haunt women's experience of themselves, despite our positive affirmations.

To deepen our understanding required looking to those feminist writers involved in exploring other possibilities, including psychoanalytic theory. These included Juliet Mitchell (1974, 1984), Jean Baker Miller (1978), Dorothy Dinnerstein (1978), Nancy Chodorow (1978, 1989), Jane Flax (1981), Carol Gilligan (1982), Luise Eichenbaum and Susie Orbach (1982), Teresa Brennan (1989), Sheila Ernst and Marie Maguire (1987), Jessica Benjamin (1990). However, whilst these writers gave us an important and varied theoretical framework from which to develop our ideas, at times we found it difficult to translate these into a working practice. It was here that we found the writings of Winnicott and Dockar-Drysdale enormously valuable.[2] A feminist perspective remains central to our work and involves attempting to identify and name the impact of sexism on women's lives, beginning at birth and their welcome into the world as female children, and their ongoing experiences as women. This perspective, including the impact of classism, is described in other papers (Trevithick, 1988, 1994).

The theme of this paper is to outline how we have adapted the work of D. W. Winnicott (1971, 1986a, 1986b, 1987, 1990) and Barbara Dockar-Drysdale (1990) into a groupwork context, together with Bion (1961), in order to address the needs of women suffering from depression.[3] However, it is important to state at the outset that whilst Winnicott is a major influence on our work, he was not particularly sympathetic to feminism. Nor do his writings adequately cover some subjects important to our exploration, such as the impact of sexism on the emotional development of girls and boys, the issue of gender identity and the construction of masculinity and femininity and the role of the father in the emotional development of the infant, the psychodynamics of domination and submission, and so on. Nevertheless, despite these gaps Winnicott's writings cover many central themes, particularly in relation to depression, and it is here that we continue to draw heavily on his work.

Theoretical framework

Within Winnicott's theoretical framework, the emotional development of the individual can be seen as a journey from dependence to independence, beginning with the absolute dependence of the new born baby, where the infant's needs must be met in an almost total way in order for the baby to move on to the next developmental stage, which is one of relative dependence where there is the beginnings of less adaptation to the needs of the infant. If all goes well at this stage, a capacity for independence begins to develop (Winnicott, 1990, p.84), though this should not be confused with premature self sufficiency, which occurs when individuals are forced into a false independence before they have the emotional resources or maturity to achieve this stage. The final stage is that of interdependence, which involves the capacity of the individual to relate to themselves, to others and to their wider environment:

> Independence is never absolute. The healthy individual does not become isolated, but becomes related to the environment in such a way that the individual and the environment can be said to be interdependent (Winnicott, 1990, p.84).

Within this developmental process, Winnicott differentiates between two types of failure: that of privation and deprivation. Privation refers to a failure within the infant's environment to facilitate the maturational process at the earliest stages of emotional development, before the infant knows about maternal care. It is the loss of a beginning, whereas deprivation is the loss of something that once was but somehow became lost or separated off, resulting in a break in the 'line-of-life' or the 'continuity of being' (Winnicott). The importance that Winnicott placed on external, cultural and environmental factors in this journey from absolute dependence to interdependence set him apart from many psychoanalysts. He stressed that it is not only the 'good-enough mother' who brings about the emotional development of the infant but also the facilitating or 'good-enough environment':

> According to this thesis a good-enough environmental provision in the earliest phase enables the infant to begin to exist, to have experience, to build a personal ego, to ride instincts, and to meet with all the difficulties inherent in life. All this feels real to the infant who becomes able to have a self...(Winnicott, 1990, p.304).

Within this 'good-enough environment' lie a range of 'cultural potentialities' which are available for individuals to take up and use, from which they could 'creatively benefit' (Benjamin, 1990, p.37). These 'potentialities' are important because they often bring about some sense of relief, some transformation, if only temporarily, from the difficulties inherent in life, particularly the anguish involved in feeling isolated and abandoned. In our work, these 'potentialities' may include women being able to call on neighbours for help or being able to utilise the local community facilities, being comforted by a particular person or object, being able to telephone me when troubled, etc. Clearly, in situations of urban decay where communities are being broken up, these 'potentialities' are fewer or more difficult to identify, and this fact must not be forgotten. However, the existence of these 'potentialities', though very important, is not in itself enough. How well people can use opportunities without feeling compromised, anxious, unreal, fragmented or exposed in some very important way in part depends on how well, particularly as children, they were carried by their parents or other adults '.. from relating to usage'.

'Object-relating' and 'use of the object' are complex concepts and refer to different aspects of experiencing through relating. In 'object-relating', '.. the subject allows certain alterations to the self to take place', whereas within the notion of 'use of the object', '...object relating is taken for granted'. Thus, the 'capacity to use the object' is essentially an inner capability because for an object to be capable of being used, it must be experienced as real (Winnicott 1971 p.88) that is, not as a projection or rooted in an omnipotent struggle for control but as something outside, independent and external. The object must also be capable of surviving attempts to destroy it, so that it is transformed from an object of fantasy (inside) to an object of reality (outside). Destruction and aggression are enlisted in this effort to differentiate and if all goes well, the relatedness will be based on '...a whole person capable of total relationships with whole persons' (Winnicott, 1987, p.220).

These theories are vitally important within social work and allied professions because they help us understand why some clients cannot take up or use the support or assistance that is on offer: if this support is not felt to be real, something tangible and permanent, then it cannot be taken up and utilised. They explain, in part, some of the intense fear and anxiety that some clients experience when seeking help, particularly for clients who have been consistently let down and failed, and highlight how frightening it can be to have to rely on other people or to trust. Some clients have been let down and criticised too often to dare believe that something positive can happen and as a result, may display difficult or unco-operative behaviour which can easily be thought of or pathologised as 'resistant' or as lacking motivation, rather than being seen as an inability to move forward or to make progress because of early failures in the transition from 'relating' to 'using'. This understanding makes the notion of empowerment and participation much more complex issues than they first appear.

Capacity to tolerate a feeling and to experience experiences

The 'depressions' experienced by the women attending our groups range from near-normal to psychotic in character (Winnicott, 1990, p.220). In order to understand where individual women lie within this range, without using psychiatric labels and diagnoses, we have found it helpful to try to identify how women relate to the life experiences they have had. At one end of the range, we work with women who have the capacity to feel, to link and reflect on their experiences, despite the pain and anguish that this evokes. In relation to this cluster of women, for whom spontaneous recovery from depression may be possible, our main task is to be as reliable and consistent in our contact as we can reasonably manage. Our aim is to get alongside women as much as we can, so that by 'living an experience together', we can reach a point where '.. the full course of an experience is allowed' (Winnicott, 1987, p.67). For Winnicott, a central theme in this work involves the concept of 'holding':

...it has as its aim not a directing of the individual's life or development, but an enabling of the tendencies which are at work within the individual, leading to a natural evolution based on growth. It is emotional growth that has been delayed and perhaps distorted, and under proper conditions the forces that would have led to growth now lead to a disentanglement of the knot (Winnicott, 1990, p.228).

By our providing a holding environment and by '...tolerating the depression until it spontaneously lifts' (Winnicott, 1986a, p.77), we hope that some transformation or change may take place. For Hannah Segal, this transformation becomes possible through distress being contained, which she describes in relation to the mother-child relationship in the following way:

When an infant has an intolerable anxiety, he (sic) deals with it by projecting it into the mother. The mother's response is to acknowledge the anxiety and do whatever is necessary to relieve the infant's distress. The infant's perception is that he has projected something intolerable into his original object, but the object was capable of containing it and dealing with it. He can then reintroject not only his original anxiety but an anxiety modified by having been contained. He also introjects an object capable of containing and dealing with anxiety. The containment of anxiety by an external object capable of understanding is a beginning of mental stability (Segal, quoted in Hinshelwood, 1991, p.248).

The containment of anxiety is, in our view, crucial if change is to take place. Where a feature of the depression is a sense of numbness or disassociation, described by Fairbairn as an 'attitude of detachment' (1952, p.6), our main focus may be to help that individual to re-experience some of the original pain or anxiety that became separated off because the feelings could not be contained or tolerated. This process of attempting to hold and contain women's emotions, particularly during periods of uncertainty, forgetfulness, flooding, provides the opportunity for women to 'sort out' and 'work through' the difference between '.. fact and fantasy or outer and inner reality' (Winnicott, 1987, p.268) thereby easing some of the impact that these painful, past experiences continue to have, which in turn allows new possibilities to emerge. According to Winnicott, dissociation is an ' .. extremely widespread defence mechanism' (1987, p.152).

Feelings of being 'unreal' and 'not whole'

However, this sorting out of fact and fantasy can be difficult for women who do not feel 'whole persons' or who feel split off or unreal to the point that they do not feel that they have had an experience. It is as if each different situation that they encounter at any one time is cocooned in a bubble, set adrift, with no connecting lines or themes to link one experience to another. These difficulties can mean that some of the women we work with are closer to privation than deprivation. As a result, some find it difficult to relate to others in the group, preferring instead to direct their comments to the groupworkers: the group dynamic frequently reflects this fragmentation. According to Bion, this inability to relate or to link comes about because the individual has '...a part-object relationship with himself (sic) as well as with objects not himself' (1959, p.311). A striking characteristic among those women who have difficulty feeling, experiencing or linking is there marked lack of curiosity:

> The disturbance of the impulse of curiosity on which all learning depends, and the denial of the mechanism by which it seeks expression, makes normal development impossible...The patient appears to have no appreciation of causation and will complain of painful states of mind while persisting in courses of action calculated to produce them (Bion, 1959, p.314).

Another noticeable characteristic is a profound sense of compliance - of 'fitting in' to whatever is required to the point that some women describe feeling that they have no 'real' personality or that they have not yet started to exist (Winnicott, 1971, p.65). There is a marked lack of aliveness, a sense of futility and limited ability or inability to recognise need or desire. Some compliance or lack of curiosity is a part of 'normal living' (Winnicott). However, what is different is the degree to which women fail to show any noticeable 'investigative attitude' (Killingmo, 1989) and the extent to which they comply and appear empty. Where women demonstrate difficulties in tolerating a feeling or in linking, our task is different and involves attempting to establish meaning. This we do verbally but also through entering the world of symbolisation and transitional phenomena in order to help bring about a regression to an earlier time in their lives, from which they can begin to have experiences and to exist. [4]

Establishing meaning

One way that we assist in the establishment of meaning involves a '...verbalisation of experiences in the immediate present', where we act more as a mirror than someone providing interpretations (Winnicott, 1971, p.118). This point is developed by Killingmo, who distinguishes between two types of therapeutic strategy:

> (1) revealing meaning and (2) establishing meaning; the first one being primarily relevant in contexts of conflict, the second in contexts of structural deficit. For the purpose of revealing meaning the relevant type of intervention is interpretation, while establishing meaning is brought about by interventions of an affirmative type (Killingmo, 1989, p. 68).

When working with people with 'structural deficit', whose sense of self appears incomplete or fragmented, Killingmo's 'affirmative interventions' include objectifying incidents or feelings to enable them to take some kind of shape or form, so that in time they can be communicated in words and shared with others; justifying in order to establish cause and effect so that they can be understood in terms of being 'reasonable natural events'; accepting in order to establish and convey the vitally important attributes of understanding and acceptance (Killingmo, 1989, p.73). It is hoped that by attempting to meet the fundamental and '.. immediate need for meaningfulness, the ego will be able to raise its level of functioning and adopt an investigating attitude - at least for a while' (Killingmo, 1989, p.73).

Putting experiences into words has also proved to be an enormously important process among deprived and disadvantaged groups of people who, perhaps as a result of class, race or gender injustices rather than failures in their emotional development may demonstrate little confidence in their capacity to think or to talk about their thoughts and feelings (Gilligan, 1982). Some have been taught to consider themselves 'stupid' or 'thick' or as 'not counting' and have internalised these negative experiences. These blows to the ego make it essential for people from deprived sections of the population to be given positive experiences, and it is here that the interventions identified by Winnicott and Killingmo are particularly important.

In addition to these interventions, we would separate out and add the importance of providing explanations about the processes that people are going through both within the group process and, if appropriate, in relation to the world and wider cultural and societal contexts. We see this as an aspect of 'maternal care', though we are careful not to inhibit women's own quest for understanding and meaning. Providing explanations can be seen as one way of attempting to contain anxieties, as well as adapting to women's individual needs, and can be particularly important for those women who, as infants, did not have events or experiences explained to them by their parents, or other adults.

Through attempting to establish meaning, which includes providing positive experiences as a 'memory of care', our hope is that in time these experiences will become assimilated into the ego to form part of the self. However, it is clear that some women do not have an 'internal hook' on to which to hang and store experiences: their sense of self or self esteem is too low to be able to internalise good experiences. This can be seen most clearly when they fail to remember positive experiences that happened in the group in previous weeks: where this is the case, our work needs to begin here. This lack of memory may be due to a range of factors (e.g. medication) but may also indicate that we have not yet been able to pitch our 'affirmative interventions' at a level where meaning could be permanently established or it could be an indicator of privation and the fact that there is insufficient emotional foundation on which to lay experiences.

It is not always clear to us why some women have little capacity to store experiences and how this came about, nor whether we can help to create a permanent 'internal hook' so that some integration can begin to take place. Yet despite these doubts, with one or two women we are involved in exploring whether some integration is possible, following the processes described by Barbara Dockar-Drysdale in relation to emotionally deprived children, but relating these to adults:

> We are thinking in terms of a series of processes which must be gone through in order to reach integration. These are experience, realization, symbolization and conceptualization. By this I mean quite simply that a child may have a good experience provided by his (sic) therapist, but that this will be of no value to him until he is able, eventually, to realize it; this is to say, to feel that this good thing really happened to him. Then he must find a way of storing the good thing inside him, which he does by means of symbolizing the experience. Last in the series of processes comes conceptualization, which is understanding intellectually what has happened to him in the course of the experience and being able to think this in words: conceptualization is only of value if it is retrospective - ideas must be the sequel to experience (Dockar-Drysdale, 1990, p.98-99).

Transitional phenomena

As part of our attempts to establish meaning, particularly among women whose experience is more deprived than privated, we also use symbolisation and transitional phenomena in order for the developmental process to start up again where it has become stuck: here we draw heavily on the work of Barbara Dockar-Drysdale. Our aim is not to fill the gaps or holes in women's emotional development, nor to push them forward prematurely, but to put a bridge across these traumas or 'impingement's' which have brought about a 'break in the line of life' (Winnicott). To achieve this, we use symbolisations as a way of reaching into women's inner reality at an earlier stage in their emotional development. Once we reach this point, we continue to use symbolisations in order to begin to provide '.. a satisfactory experience which must somehow have been missing at the beginning' (Dockar-Drysdale, 1990, p.46).

Although most of this transitional work takes place on an individual basis within a counselling relationship, we do use some of the same processes in our groupwork. We mainly do this through 'adaptation to need', which involves setting up a situation where we attempt to meet the unique needs of each individual woman. Sometimes, this may involve making women a particular drink upon arrival at Womankind, or supplying a certain type of biscuit. Other times, it may involve women identifying something that they would like us to give to them. For example, one woman asked me to give her a hankie which she always carries with her, another wears a scarf, one hugs a soft blanket during the group. Another carries and regularly loses a particular stone, using the metaphor of being lost to communicate with us and we reply using the same metaphor. Many carry cards that I and other workers have written to them over the years, one woman has a hug each week, another wants to hear certain words of reassurance, and so forth.

For some, being given objects or gestures in this way can help to bring about a partial or 'localised regression' (Dockar-Drysdale, 1990). This is spontaneous, in the sense that it is not a conscious choice, and often takes the form of women feeling very defenceless and childlike. They describe needing someone to take care of them, to feed and clothe them and, most importantly, to explain and interpret the world for them. Sometimes, women in this state retreat to bed, because the effort involved in surviving takes up all their energy or because the world is too bewildering to cope with. However, because the regression is partial, most are still able to undertake the demands made of them in their everyday lives and can manage to get to the group: we pay for taxis if it becomes too difficult to travel.

Once women begin to develop the capacity for storing and

reflecting upon experiences, it is hoped that two changes will occur. Firstly, that in time they will use the experience of being contained to become the containers of their own inner reality. Secondly, once some confidence has been gained and internalised, that their dependency upon the groupworkers, and Womankind, will become less because a different internal order has been created:

.. the individual acquires an internal environment...(and)...thus becomes able to find new situation-holding experiences, and is able in time to take over the function of the situation-holding person for someone else, without resentment (Winnicott, 1987, p. 271).

This transition from contained to container is vitally important for those women who are mothers because it means that they are developing the capacity to be the 'situation-holding person' for their children. However, it must again be stressed that for this to happen requires more than individual endeavour or the capacity to 'use the object'. It also requires an environmental setting that is sensitive to women's needs and capable of providing experiences that are nourishing, fulfilling and energising. Where these external facilitating factors do not exist, women have little choice but to dwell in the isolated and 'false' realm of compliance, premature self sufficiency and secrecy.

Groupwork

In order to put our work into context, the following is a description of the cross section of women currently attending our groups and how we see our approach in relation to the groupwork being practiced within social work. The paper then goes on to describe a typical group.

Cross section of women attending our groups

The following breakdown is based on the findings of a pilot study undertaken in 1994. Each group is made up of nine women. Of these 27 women, four are black (Afro Caribbean) and three come from other ethnic minority groups (all the groupworkers are white women). Their age range spans 22-65 years, with half being under 30. Between them, they have had 36 children, of whom 14 are under ten years old. A small number of women are married but most live alone on benefits: only one woman works part-time in paid employment. Poverty, isolation and loneliness are very real and worrying issues for almost all the women we see.

The majority of women speak of being depressed for many years, some being unable to recall any period when they felt otherwise. Their despair is profound and over half have attempted suicide at some time in their lives: in the case of two women, their mothers and a brother actually committed suicide. Interestingly, only about one third of the women we see have been admitted to a psychiatric hospital: more have been treated in day hospitals or day centres. This is significant given the fact that the majority would be classified as suffering from 'severe' or 'enduring' mental health problems: over half have been diagnosed as schizophrenic or as borderline psychotic. (We do not use medical diagnoses, preferring instead to use the word depression because this is how most women describe themselves). Almost all are taking some kind of psychotropic (mood altering) drug, mainly anti-depressants, but also minor and major tranquillisers. An analysis of our referrals revealed that 42 per cent came from General Practitioners (family doctors) and 34 per cent from social workers and other health workers.

Groupwork within social work

There is considerable concern that groupwork is being practiced less than it once was within social work and that where it does exist, it tends to be without a clear theoretical base and to be focused on certain client groups (women and young offenders) rather than available to all (McCaughan, 1988). The reasons for this fall-off in groupwork are many: it has proved difficult for some social work academics, managers and practitioners to acknowledge the value and importance of groupwork as a social work method and to take this viewpoint forward; the allocation of resources and priorities within area teams can mitigate against groupwork; some practitioners leave social work courses feeling insufficiently trained, skilled and committed to undertake groupwork; there can be an absence of appropriate supervision and support; there is a question about whether the groupwork theories and practices currently being used are effective in providing support for clients and for bringing about change, and so on. Another reason put forward is that groupwork may require a different more collaborative and participative style of working (McCaughan, 1988, p.86), and this may be difficult to achieve amid the daily pressures and tensions involved in many fieldwork settings, particularly statutory work.

Whilst this may be an accurate description, it places our groupwork approach outside social work because we are pre-occupied with different issues and choose to deal with these in a different way. Although our closest professional links lie with social work, it is difficult to categorise our work because we are drawing our theoretical framework, training and supervision from different sources to those normally available. Some would describe our approach as being closer to 'casework in a group' than to 'real groupwork' (Kurland and Salmon, 1993). However, this issue is less important to us than whether we are being effective in meeting the needs of the women who seek our help: this is very difficult to measure and evaluate.

Central to our work is a belief in the importance of self determination, which for us involves constantly reviewing and modifying our groupwork approach so that by 'adapting to need', women can begin to find their own way, in their own time, to whatever personal goal(s) they have set themselves. Within this framework, our emphasis is to provide an approach that will meet the needs of a deprived, disadvantaged and depressed cross section of women. In some ways, this pre-occupation has kept us from having to address the tensions and rivalries that continue to exist within groupwork in relation to one-to-one work (sometimes described as casework) and community work. It has also meant that we have failed to challenge creatively the orthodoxy described by authors such as Kurland and Salmon in what they define as 'real groupwork' (1993, p.10). Yet we are deeply committed to encouraging the development of a range of different groupwork approaches and believe that unless we can encourage flexibility and experimentation within social work, we run the risk of becoming 'territorially defensive', isolated, theoretically adrift and unable to allow for innovation or collaboration in inter-professional initiatives currently under way (Heap, 1992).

The role of the groupworkers

Each depression group has three workers: two group leaders and a group co-ordinator, with each undertaking different roles. The group co-ordinator has the centrally important task of ensuring that Womankind provides a setting, a 'transitional space' (Winnicott) that can act as a bridge from which women can begin to explore their thoughts and feelings, '...the chance to remember in...(their)...own way and time.' (Winnicott, 1971, p.xii). The aim is to create a 'good-enough environmental provision', a 'setting that gives confidence', from which women can begin to reveal themselves to themselves. According to Bollas, the existence of a holding environment acts as an 'invitation' for an individual to regress (Bollas, 1986, p.94). The group co-ordinator also provides the continuity between one group and the next by making brief notes each week on the group process and any follow up work required. These notes are then read out when we meet before the group. However, recently we have begun to explore Bion's stance of leaving aside anything that is already known about an individual or the group, in order to keep the focus not on '...what has happened nor with what is going to happen but with what is happening' (Bion, 1967, p.272).

During the group, the co-ordinator mainly acts as an observer, though it is often her task to accompany women who walk out of the group. It is the task of the group leaders to aid communication within the group, which involves enabling members to '... encompass what is known or become aware of it with acceptance' (Winnicott, 1971, p.102), based on the premise that it is '...the patient and only the patient who has the answers'. In order for group members to feel this acceptance, our approach is one where we play an active part in providing some of the care which, to a large extent, continues to be absent in women's lives. This is based on Winnicott's concept that '...cure at its root means care' (1986a, p.112), where 'care-cure' is seen as part of the concept of holding. Thus, as groupworkers we become:

...one who responds to need, that is to say, of adaptation, concern and reliability, of cure in the sense of care...This carries no sense of superiority (Winnicott, 1986a, p.116).

As groupworkers, it can sometimes be difficult to maintain this caring, maternal approach, particularly when we are being provoked to retaliate, to be clever or to give up, either because of our own personal histories or as a result of women's need to re-enact earlier failures. Here it is important that we have a theoretical framework from which to understand ourselves and other women's reactions and behaviour. The high priority given to supervision is essential in helping us to bear women's anxieties and to maintain professional boundaries. There is an expectation that all groupworkers will attend as many supervision sessions as possible and that group leaders will be in group or individual therapy themselves.

In order to provide anonymity and to protect confidentiality, the following account is not a description of any one group but an amalgamation. All names have been changed. However, the comments and encounters described actually occurred. Prior to the group session about to be described, there has been a brief meeting between Norma Wilson, the co-leader, Lesley Bradley, the group co-ordinator, and myself to hear a resume of the main issues raised in the group the previous week and to discuss any new developments.

The group

'Here we go again,' murmurs Janice, as she drags herself up the stairs behind me, her black boots stamping her misery into every step.

'Why do you come if you hate it so much?' comes a question from someone further down the stairs.

'Because there's nowhere else to go, is there?' snaps Janice, who by now has arrived in the groupwork room and thrown herself on a pile of cushions in the corner.

Joan is next to arrive: she settles herself in the centre of a pile of cushions and kicks her shoes off. She looks comfortable. As much as possible, we have tried to make the groupwork room a warm, soft and soothing place to be. Pastel colours predominate and there is an abundance of cushions of every size. On the walls are paintings and photographs that women have brought in and on the shelves are other symbolic objects - a shell, a box, a little clay figurine, a flower, a teddy bear. The presence of these symbolic objects is important because they indicate that some women are beginning to explore and use the transitional space that Womankind provides.

By now the groupwork room is beginning to fill up as seven of the nine participants settle themselves down for another weekly one and a half hour session of the group. Once this is done, I begin by welcoming everyone and by saying that we have had apologies from Linda and Michelle who cannot come this week. I then ask whether anyone wants to start, perhaps to say something about how they feel about Linda and Michelle being away, how they are feeling now, or how the week has been for them. A silence prevails and I and the other groupworkers use this as an opportunity to sense the mood of the group and its individual members. I pick up a feeling of apprehension and my eyes turn to Janice, who by now has buried her head between her legs, and is gently rocking herself backwards and forwards.

I ask Janice what's the matter, what has happened to make her feel that she did not want to come to the group today? She does not reply except to bury her head even deeper.

The room is full of silence and almost in a whisper I ask, 'what's happening .. why do you need to hide away today, Janice? Can you put words to your feelings?' She is visibly struggling to find words.

'It's so hard...so hard to get here...the journey is too difficult. I feel so scared all the time .. sometimes trying to get to the group feels like cycling over Everest...' She begins to cry, quietly.

There is some shuffling in the group: a box of tissues is passed along and acts as a welcome distraction. In an attempt to give comfort and reassurance, Alice puts her hand on Janice's knee. This produces further tears:

'I think I've made her worse' says Alice, despairingly.

'No Alice', replies Norma, 'she just needs to cry, but I'm wondering how you are feeling?'

'Awful...absolutely terrible. I can't stand this...all this misery and depression: it's too much. I wasn't as bad as this before I started coming to the group...I was alright really...'.

'How can you say that?' interrupts Joan, kindly. 'You never used to go out, except to the doctors or back and forwards into hospital. How can you say that you were alright?'

'I just had my own pain then, nobody else's...I can't stand this. It's too much to bear...all this misery...'

With these words Alice rushes out of the room. Lesley follows to ensure that she has someone with her and that she does not leave the building in a distressed state.

The mood of the group feels worried and startled, prompting Norma to ask how they feel about Alice's departure. The question is met with silence. We know that if left too long, silence can be experienced as persecutory and can fragment the group. Yet despite this, we decide to wait.

> Elizabeth, who finds silences difficult, is the first to speak: her voice cuts through the silence like an explosion as she shouts: 'I wish I could walk out like that but you've got to keep going, you've got to think positively haven't you? Otherwise no-one will want to know you and you're left with nothing'.

Her smile is full of apprehension and compliance, as if searching for approval, and my mind drifts back to the previous week where she relayed comments from her clinical psychologist on the importance of positive thinking as a strategy for dealing with her depression.

Another silence prevails. The tension mounts, particularly for Elizabeth, whose shuffling is becoming more pronounced.

> After a while Norma asks: 'Elizabeth, I wonder whether you felt angry at Alice for walking out?'
> 'No, not really'.
> 'When you say 'not really', what do you mean?'
> 'I don't know'.
> 'Well then, I'm wondering whether you feel you need to be positive

when you come to the group?'

'No, I like coming to the group but I just keep thinking 'why me, why am I always in the wrong, why am I always to blame?' When my husband divorced me, he got everything. I just had a bag of clothes and nothing else. No house, no money, no friends, nothing...and eight years later, look what I've got...nothing'.

Elizabeth cannot yet cry. Instead she expresses her discomfort and pain through repetitive alterations to her charity shop clothes. She appears confused and, sensing this, Norma asks whether Elizabeth would like to say some more about the difficulties she experiences in managing her life and keeping going. She declines the invitation, preferring instead to return to her own thoughts and memories.

In anticipation of the conversation between Elizabeth and Norma continuing, another silence falls on the group.

This is broken by a comment from Joan: 'Well, if no-one else wants to speak, I'd like to say that I had a better week. I didn't feel so terrified or panicky, though I'm scared that it will come back'.

'What will come back?' I ask.

'This feeling that everything is falling apart, that I'm going to fall down a big deep hole and be forgotten...forever...left to rot. What I don't understand, and it worries me, is why do I suddenly feel so awful... so anxious? What happens to make me feel so young, so small... defenceless...empty...frightened...like something terrible is going to happen but I don't know what. Do you know?' Joan turns to me and indicates that she wants an answer.

I feel uncertain about whether to reply but decide to. 'Well, I think that over the past few weeks your defences have not been working as well as they have in the past. This seemed to begin about the time that we closed the group to new women .. is that right?' Joan nods. 'Since then, you have seemed very vulnerable and frightened, as if you've tumbled or fallen into another time, an earlier time in your life, and you want someone to take care of you'. She beings to cry and I ask if she wants me to stop. She shakes her head. 'You've been talking more and more about how tired you are of caring for others and that you want someone to take care of you, to comfort you, to tell you that everything will be alright.

My guess is that you have felt these feelings before, perhaps around the time when you were admitted to hospital?' Joan nods and so too do some of the other women in the group. 'Maybe one reason why you feel so awful is because you became aware of your own neediness and your desire to be taken care of and I think that this frightened you. But the fact that you can now feel this neediness is important because it can mean that the developmental process is beginning to start up again...that you are beginning to sort out and work through some of the deprivation and neglect that you experienced in childhood'. She nods again: 'I feel I haven't started to live yet. I haven't had a life...I look alive but I'm dead inside...dead...I've tried to be good...but that's not the same as being alive. Everything feels pointless...futile...'. She begins to sob deeply.

Once again the group is silent. I recall a phone call I had to my home one weekend where I asked Joan if she needed something from me to help her cope during this difficult time. She identified a pillow - a blue pillow and as fate would have it, I found just the right pillow some days after. I am not sure how I knew it to be the right one, but my hunch was confirmed when I gave it to Joan. It now travels wherever she goes and she says it is a source of great comfort.

After some time has passed, Norma asks whether my comments relate to other women's experiences and some begin to tell their own, painful stories.

Tina's comments focus on her experiences of being psychotic in her adolescence and how she now connects this to early childhood experiences of sexual and physical abuse. Her words speak to Janice's experiences of abuse: she is now sitting up, listening intently. Elizabeth follows by describing how she never felt she matched up to her parents' expectations of her. This comment serves to remind Tina and Janice of how much they too felt unwanted and unloved as children.

'My dad told me I was a mistake and that's how I've been treated all my life', recalls Tina.

Janice nods her understanding. Thinking back on Tina's life, the picture I have is of no-one setting a place for her at the family table. Instead, I see her hanging around - waiting and hoping for some scraps of food, of affection to be thrown her way: she re-enacts this feeling of unimportance in the group and we have to be vigilant not to forget her. My minds drifts to Janice, whom I see as a lost but capable child, who is expected to find her own way home. Though there are signposts and milestones, maps and helpful guides, she does not know how to read or use them. Instead, she is left feeling that life is a huge struggle, like 'cycling over Everest', sometimes without pedals.

Another silence: women look lost in their own thoughts, as if grief stricken. My mind drifts to the meaning of the word 'stupid', which originally meant 'numbed with grief'. My preoccupation, and theirs, is disturbed by Alice returning to the group, looking relaxed and calm, followed by Lesley. However, Alice quickly becomes worried by the atmosphere and asks whether she has come back into the group at the wrong time. I reassure her and ask whether she knows why she had to leave the group at that point.

'No, I just had to go.'
Catching a sense of lostness, I ask her how it feels to be back: 'I don't know. I don't feel I've arrived back yet'.
'Is there anything we can do to help you to get back into the group?'
'No. I just don't feel all here but I'm alright. Can you talk to someone else?'

She is beginning to become agitated, so I decide to leave the issue there.

In the silence that ensues, my thoughts turn to Sheila, who has rarely spoken in the group since she joined over a year ago. Though clearly attentive to what is being said, she has not yet found it possible to entrust her thoughts and feelings to the group. She carries a terrifying fear of 'going mad', and much of her life is spent trying to find the right balance in the face of conflicting internal and external pressures. She has great difficulty recognising any feelings, positive or negative, and finds it almost impossible to let anyone get close to her, including her little children. So far, our approach has been to adapt to Sheila's needs as much as we can, which includes not putting her under any pressure to speak in the group. Our most intense work is undertaken in the counselling sessions which Sheila attends each week.

My thoughts are broken by an angry outburst from Jenny who, turning to me, asks: 'Are you going to ask how my week has been...do you care? Well, it's been absolutely awful and coming here is no help at all. I feel as unwanted here as I feel everywhere else'.

'Why do you say that?' I ask.

'You're all the same. I know I ask for it, but you're as bad as all the others who've let me down'.

'In what way do you think I have let you down?'

'When I was in hospital, no-one came to see me, not even you. I was just left to sort everything out for myself, yet you went to see Elizabeth when she was admitted...oh, it doesn't matter. What's done is done. There's no point in talking about it now, so go on to someone else', and with these words, she waves her hand, as if dismissing me.

I ask Jenny what would help her to work through her feeling of being abandoned by me but she hears my question as attacking and, as a result, it elicits no response. Although her silence feels uncomfortable, I am aware that once Jenny feels ready, she will find words for her feelings, but that this process cannot be rushed.

In the time remaining, the discussion moves around from one topic to another and as much as they can, women strive to keep some kind of balance between trying to have some time and attention for themselves, whilst also allowing space for other women to speak. Given the degree of depression and deprivation within the group, there is an amazing amount of generosity, tolerance and patience for each woman's individual struggle. Such generosity can be interpreted as a form of self denial, masochism or as an inability to manage negative, envious or rivalrous feelings. It can also be '...a curious way of mourning and caring for the damaged parts' of themselves (Bollas, 1987, p.243), which cannot yet be contacted or communicated. My own view is that a profound fear of criticism and 'getting it wrong' also influences whether women will or will not take up the space.

Eventually, an hour and a half has passed and we wind up the group.

After the group

Once this is done, women leave the groupwork room to have coffee and tea in the kitchen. The kitchen then becomes their 'own space', a second therapeutic experience. It is here that women make contact with one another, perhaps to arrange to meet during the week or to talk over the telephone. We play no part in these arrangements except occasionally to unravel, within the group, conflicts or misunderstanding that may have arisen. Some women feel uneasy about making social contact in this way and worry that they don't know how to be sociable or that confidentiality may be breached. Some feel tentative because the memory of earlier disappointments and betrayals of trust remain fresh in their minds. Despite these concerns, on the whole most women handle this contact well.

Relating theory to practice

Meanwhile, Lesley, Norma and I meet for the second time to compare observations on the group process, to discuss women's individual contributions and how we ourselves are currently feeling. In terms of countertransference, we attempt to distinguish between feelings that are in response to group members and those emotions which intrude into the work from our own past (Heimann, 1950). This is also a time when we attempt to link theory to practice. We begin by noting that for Jenny, I continue to be a 'reliable hate object' (Dockar-Drysdale, 1990). Having been taken to the 'point of failure' in the therapeutic alliance by failing to visit her in hospital, I now stand alongside others from the past who have failed her (Winnicott, 1990, p.258). My task is to withstand and survive Jenny's continued attacks and not to retaliate or abandon her. The issue of hatred, like women's fears and fantasies, is a complex issue which cannot be explored in detail here except to ask what are these feelings being used to convey - as groupworkers, who are we becoming and how are we being used?

Our work with Joan has provided us with an opportunity to see whether a partial or 'localised regression' is possible and beneficial in a groupwork setting and so far, this appears to be case, particularly where women's primary experience is one of deprivation and not privation. This was the situation for Joan who throughout her childhood was expected to be compliant and to subsume her needs to those of others. A psychotic breakdown after the birth of her first baby, resulted in her admission to hospital, where she was given ECT and since that time, 20 years ago, she has been struggling to recover from recurring severe bouts of depression and to 'feel alright about herself'.

Her regression took her back to being a young child and revived a neediness that terrified her. She was haunted by a fear, an 'unthinkable anxiety' (Winnicott), which she could not describe in words beyond saying that she felt trapped, as if she had to be on the move for fear of being caught. Our approach was to encourage her to identify what she could cope with and to try to keep her within this range. For some depressed women, it can be almost impossible to be still, to 'be' rather than to 'do', particularly when gripped by anxiety. We also encouraged her to talk to her family and friends as much as she could, though at times this proved difficult because it exposed her in ways which made her feel vulnerable and frightened. During this period, she was able to 'use' me more, by writing and phoning me at home, which provided her with some of the holding that she needed. Though we could only provide limited help, what was important to Joan, and other women have said the same, was that as much as we could, we were willing to be with her in the dark pit into which she had fallen. She also felt comforted by our efforts to explain what we saw happening to her, which is something that she rarely experienced in childhood, but very much yearned for and needed.

After about four weeks, Joan emerged from this crisis, and since then has continued to explore those parts of herself that became hidden in childhood. According to Winnicott, as long as the individual is located in a 'facilitating environment' from which development is possible, the development process can start up again at any time. Other indicators might be the birth of curiosity or flashes of spontaneous, uninhibited behaviour. For Barbara Dockar-Drysdale, one way to evaluate whether the developmental process has been revived is when an individual is able to identify 'the feeling of need and the desire for satisfaction'. Joan is in touch with her needs, which are to be herself and to be free of the anxieties and inhibitions that stop her from enjoying life. In this sense she is searching for her true self:

> The spontaneous gesture is the True Self in action. Only the True Self can be creative and only the True Self can feel real. Whereas a True Self feels real, the existence of a False Self results in a feeling unreal or a sense futility.

> The False Self, if successful in its function, hides the True Self, or else finds a way of enabling the True Self to start to live. Such an outcome may be achieved by all manner of means, but we observe most closely those instances in which the sense of things being real or worth while arrives during a treatment (Winnicott, 1990, p.148).

Many of the women we work with are reluctant to look at difficult feelings or to allow themselves to have an experience in case they are hurt again. This is particularly true of Janice, Tina and Sheila. Their childhood experiences of abuse have left them, in different ways, deeply scarred and, as a result, they carry a profound anxiety that they will 'fall apart' or be further traumatised if they are pushed to remember before they feel emotionally ready or prepared (Trevithick 1993). Here again, our task involves being able to reassure, to 'hold together the threads of experience' (Winnicott), to contain anxieties, to explain events (where appropriate) and to show a willingness to help. It also involves pitching our interventions at the correct level and then to wait '...until the patient tells us...if we make the interpretation out of our own cleverness and experience then the patient must refuse it or destroy it' (Winnicott, 1990, p.182).

Like Joan, Janice is in a state of partial regression and, as a result, is finding it hard to deal with those aspects of her life that require her to be an adult. Nevertheless, she does manage to get herself to the group each week. Janice's reference to 'cycling over Everest' is a part of an ongoing communication using metaphors connected to journeys. According to Barbara Dockar-Drysdale, the use of metaphor in this way acts as a safeguard against an individual being further traumatised because if the metaphor is poorly chosen, inappropriate or untimely, it is likely to be experienced as irrelevant or confusing rather than traumatising.

Tina's current difficulties take a different form to those of Janice. Her days are dominated by flashbacks of deeply disturbing scenes, some of which she cannot bear to relate. She also suffers from recurring nightmares where she is being chased, caught and punished in some way. When these flashbacks become too difficult to bear, which often happens at night, she sometimes rings me at home. Containing her anxiety in this way helps her to feel less alone. Her fear of having another breakdown is very profound and leaves us feeling that in addition to the psychotic episode in adolescence, she may have had other breakdowns earlier in her life (Winnicott, 1986b).

Our thoughts turn to Alice whose tendency to split means that although she is there in person, she is able to describe very clearly the sense that some part of her is missing from the group. Her own sense of being fragmented is, for the most part, how she experiences the group, which raises questions about what part she and others bring to the group and how these are played out. This in turn raises a more general question about the role of the group in meeting individual needs and how this relates to the '...interplay between individual needs, group mentality and culture' (Bion, 1961, p.55).

In relation to Elizabeth, we felt that this week, we failed to pitch our interventions at a level that conveyed sufficient understanding and acceptance and, as a result, she was unable to communicate her feelings or to make links. However, some of this difficulty may be due to her poor nutrition or emotional exhaustion. Elizabeth's life is very hard and this fact alone can make communication difficult: 'People in pain cannot concentrate' (Klein, 1990, p.40). Surviving from day to day takes up almost all of her physical and emotional energy and on many occasions she has come to the group feeling 'ready to throw in the towel'. An attempted suicide last year brought home to us the depth of her despair and how pointless life can be when the central, overriding experience is one of isolation and loneliness. Elizabeth is one of a handful of women who could be described as having a 'deficit pathology'. Her main purpose in coming to the group is not to work through and sort out painful experiences but to have somewhere to go each week where she will be cared for and nurtured. Whilst this need is legitimate, and forms part of our overall approach, it can create tensions within the group because Elizabeth is often not prepared to discuss her feelings beyond a certain point. Among the groupworkers, her situation causes concern because we are aware that she needs more practical and emotional care than we are currently able to provide. Elizabeth and Alice come across as suffering more from privation and both have been diagnosed as schizophrenic.

With regard to Sheila, we discussed whether we are doing enough to create the opportunity for her to find words. Sheila is 25 years old, has three small sons under seven and lives in a run-down housing estate in one of the poorest areas of Bristol. For the past year, she has seen someone from Womankind for one-to-one counselling and it is not clear whether this contact interferes with her ability to speak in the group. She feels it does not and insists that she 'gets a lot out of coming', even if she cannot speak. Whilst silence can be used as a defence, we are aware that people communicate in different ways and that '...significant relating and communicating is silent' (Winnicott, 1990, p.184). In addition to Sheila's silence, what is noticeable is her marked lack of curiosity, which is a concern that the school have also identified in relation to her sons. However, in recent months there has been some changes, particularly in her ability to seek help and to share her concerns with others ('use of the object'). For example, Sheila is beginning to have contact with other mothers, and to communicate her worries about the children to their fathers and at the school. These developments may be an indication that Sheila is starting to become the 'situation-holding person' for her sons and whilst she finds it frightening to expose her needs, she uses her counselling sessions well to give her support and encouragement. One day, we hope she will be able to use the group in the same way.

Conclusion

At this stage, we are not clear whether our approach is helpful to women whose experience is more privated than deprived, beyond offering kindness, concern and somewhere to go each week. However, we are clear that one of the greatest difficulties we encounter is in trying to meet the needs of women across this range within the same group. A detailed discussion of this issue goes beyond the scope of this paper except to say that until we adopt different selection procedures, our groupwork approach will always be some kind of a compromise between the needs of women who fall somewhere between 'neurotic' and 'psychotic' forms of depressions, between different manifestations of deprivation and privation respectively.

By choosing to emphasise how we have applied the writings of Winnicott and Dockar-Drysdale to our groupwork with depressed women, I am aware that I have not covered other crucial issues such as those relating to group dynamics and processes, particularly the use we make of transference and countertranference phenomena, projection, projective identification and other defence mechanisms, how we evaluate the effectiveness of our approach, how we cope with differences across the groups and among the groupworkers, our use of transitional phenomena, the supervision and training we receive, and so forth. Hopefully, some of these issues will be discussed in detail in papers yet to be written.

Instead I have described how we have used and adapted psychoanalytic concepts, particularly the work of Winnicott and Barbara Dockar-Drysdale, in order to develop an approach that is rooted in our feminism and our desire to enable women to relate better to themselves, to other women, to other people, and to their wider environment. If to experience is to exist, then one of our tasks can be to provide experiences within a groupwork setting, a meal, from which women can take in and digest sensations, both good and bad, so that in their emptiness and hunger, they can begin to feed, and to feel filled up.

The emotional starvation I have described is not confined to the women we work with. I believe this problem also exists within social work where many clients have been, for a variety of reasons, deprived of the food and nourishment necessary to live creatively and to move forward. For some, this results in an inability to function without a degree of dependency and support. Although dependency is being discouraged more and more within social work, social workers and their clients are likely to fail in their efforts to make progress if these needs remain unacknowledged and misunderstood. In our work with depressed, deprived and disadvantaged women, who mirror the abilities and difficulties that many social work clients present (Sheppard, 1993), it is important that our work starts at the correct point - namely at the point where clients feel 'together' and 'whole' enough to meet and cope with the difficulties that they are being asked to address. Where people present themselves as being too fragmented and 'untogether' to achieve this, our work needs to start there, which requires learning how to help individuals to pick up the fragments of experience, existence and personhood so that in time, a 'whole person' capable of tolerating a 'whole experience' may eventually emerge. Where this is not possible, and a clear inability to manage the world and its complexities has been acknowledged, particularly by the individual concerned, we feel that as a society it is our moral responsibility to provide a range of alternatives, including residential settings, where vulnerable people can be sheltered from the unmanageable strains and stresses of life.

Groupwork provides an important dimension for understanding that vulnerability because it provides an opportunity to observe how individuals relate to one another, to themselves and to people invested with authority, status and power (in our case, group leaders). Without this knowledge, our understanding of human beings can only be partial. In our experience, groupwork can also provide a very important opportunity from which individuals can begin to describe and identify their personal capabilities and needs. Here we see the group as a base from which people can begin to explore and extend whatever cultural and environmental possibilities that lie within their reach but beyond their vision.

This paper was presented to the Third Women's Issues Symposium at the Graduate School of Social Work, University of Houston, Texas, 19 February 1994.

Acknowledgements

I would like to thank Barbara Dockar-Drysdale, Phyllida Parsloe, Robert French, Joanna Ryan, Allan Brown, Judy Carver, Kate Lyon, Brian Caddick,

Russ Vince, Joan Solomon, Lesley Bradley, Eva Gell, Norma Wilson, Carla Keogh, Sheila Ernst and Jill Brown for their helpful comments and corrections.

Notes

1. In addition to running three depression groups, Womankind provides a range of services that include some individual counselling, a telephone helpline, an out-of-hours telephone line for evenings and weekends, a befriending scheme based in a local psychiatric hospital, a volunteer programme, placements for social work students, regular talks and training workshops for practitioners working with depressed men and women.

2. The late Donald Winnicott was a paediatrician, psycho-analyst and twice President of the British Psycho-Analytic Society. Barbara Dockar-Drysdale is a psychotherapist and the founder of the Mulberry Bush School for children needing residential psychotherapeutic care. She was for many years a Consultant Psychotherapist to the Cotswold Community for disturbed and deprived adolescent boys and currently acts as a consultant at Womankind.

3. In some ways, the task we have set ourselves is similar to that of Bion (1961 p. 143) except that instead of drawing on the work of Klein, as Bion did, we are using the work of Winnicott and Dockar-Drysdale to help us to understand the 'emotional life' of the individual and of the group.

4. It may be helpful to describe in greater detail what is meant by the terms transitional object and symbols or symbolisation. Symbols can be both conscious and unconscious. For Rycroft, the latter represent '...an unconscious substitution of one image, idea, or activity for another...a private construction...' (Rycroft, 1968, pp.162-63).

    For Winnicott, transitional objects (piece of blanket, etc.) mark the infant's '...progress towards experiencing' (1971, p.6). They act as a soother more than a comforter because they are '...more important than the mother, an almost inseparable part of the infant' (Winnicott, 1971, p.7):

    ...when we witness an infant's employment of a transitional

object, the first not-me possession, we are witnessing both the child's first use of a symbol and the first experience of play... The use of an object symbolises the union of two now separate things, baby and mother, at the point in time and space of the initiation of their state of separateness (Winnicott, 1971, pp.96-97).

Initially, when we ask women to symbolise their past experiences through the use of an object, we do not always know, nor do women themselves know, whether the object will take on the significance of a transitional object - whether it will become 'inseparable part' of the woman and carried at all times. Hence, the objects in the groupwork room are primarily symbolisations. As a symbol or a transitional object, (a rabbit, a cushion, stones, panda, paintings, photographs, etc.) it is hoped that they begin a process that involves returning to the individual those sensations, feelings and experiences that have somehow become lost or separated off.

References

Brennan, T. (1989) (ed.) Between Feminism and Psychoanalysis. London: Routledge.

Benjamin, B. (1990) The Bonds of Love. London: Virago.

Bion, W.R. (1961) Experiences in Groups. London: Tavistock/Routledge.

Bion, W.R. (1959) 'Attacks on linking', International Journal of Psychoanalysis, 40, pp.308-15).

Bion, W.R. (1967) 'Notes on memory and desire', Psycho-Analytic Forum, II(3), pp.271-80.

Bollas, C. (1986) 'The transformational object' in The British School of Psychoanalysis: The Independent Tradition. London: Free Association Books.

Bollas, C. (1987) The Shadow of the Object: Psychoanalysis of the Unthought Known. London: Free Association Books.

Chodorow, N. (1978) The Reproduction of Mothering: Psychoanalysis and the Sociology of Gender. Berkeley: University of California Press.

Chodorow, N. (1989) Feminism and Psychoanalytic Theory. London: Yale University Press.

Dinnerstein, D. (1978) The Rocking of the Cradle. London: Souvenir Press.

Dockar-Drysdale, B. (1990) The Provision of Primary Experience: Winnicottian Work with Children. London: Free Association Books.

Eichenbaum, L. and Orbach, S. (1982) Outside In: Inside Out. Harmondsworth: Penguin Books.

Ernst, S. and Maguire, M. (eds.) (1987) Living With the Sphinx: Papers from the London Women's Therapy Centre. London: Women's Press.

Fairbairn, W.R. (1952) Psychoanalytic Studies of the Personality. London: Routledge & Kegan Paul.

Flax, J. (1981) 'The conflict between nurturance and autonomy in mother-daughter relationships and within feminism' in Elisabeth Howell and Marjorie Bayes (eds.) Women and Mental Health. New York: Basic Books.

Gilligan, C. (1982) In a Different Voice: Psychological Theory and Women's Development. Cambridge: Harvard University Press.

Heap, K. (1992) 'The European groupwork scene: where were we? where are we? where are we going?', Groupwork, 5(1), pp.9-22.

Heimann, P. (1950) 'On counter-transference', International Journal of Psycho-Analysis, 31, pp.81-84.

Hinshelwood, R.D. (1991) A Dictionary of Kleinian Thought. London: Free Association Books.

Killingmo, B. (1989) 'Conflict and deficit: implications for technique', International Journal of Psycho-Analysis, 70, pp.65-79.

Klein, J. (1990) 'Patients who are not ready for interpretations', British Journal of Psychotherapy, 7(1), pp.38-49.

Kurland, R. and Salmon, R. (1993) 'Groupwork versus casework in a group', Groupwork, 6(1), pp.5-16.

McCaughan, N. (1988) 'Swimming upstream: a survey of articles on groupwork in social work journals 1986-87', Groupwork, 1, pp.77-89.

Miller, J.B. (1978) Towards a New Psychology of Women. Harmondsworth: Penguin Books.

Mitchell, J. (1974) Psychoanalysis and Feminism. Harmondsworth: Penguin Books.

Mitchell, J. (1984) Women: The Longest Revolution. London: Virago.

Rycroft, R. (1968) A Critical Dictionary of Psychoanalysis. Harmondsworth: Penguin Books.

Sheppard, M. (1993) 'Maternal depression and childcare: the significance for social work and social research', Adoption & Fostering, 17(2).

Trevithick, P. (1988) 'Unconsciousness raising with working class women' in Krzowski, S. and Land, P. (eds.) In Our Experience: Workshops at the Women's Therapy Centre. London: Women's Press.

Trevithick, P. (1993) 'Surviving childhood sexual and physical abuse: the experience of two women of Irish-English parentage' in Ferguson, H., Gilligan, R. and Torode, R. (eds.) Surviving Childhood Adversity: Issues for Policy and Practice. Dublin: Social Studies Press.

Trevithick, P. (1994) 'We've Come Too Far To Give Up Now': Feminism and Psychodynamic theory'. An Unpublished Paper Presented at the Third Women's Symposium at the Graduate School of Social Work, University of Houston Texas on February 19th, 1994.

Winnicott, D.W. (1971) Playing and Reality. London: Routledge.

Winnicott, D.W. (1986a) Home is Where We Start From. Harmondsworth: Penguin.

Winnicott, D.W. (1986b) 'Fear of breakdown' in Kohon, G. (ed.) The British School of Psychoanalysis: The Independent Tradition. London: Free Association Books.

Winnicott, D.W. (1987) Through Paediatrics to Psychoanalysis. London: Hogarth.

Winnicott, D.W. (1990) The Maturational Process and the Facilitating Environment. London: Karnac Books.

This chapter was first published in 1995 in *Groupwork* Vol. 8(1), pp.5-33

At the time of writing, Pamela Trevithick was a part-time Lecturer in Social Work at the University of Bristol, and a Groupwork Practitioner and Counsellor at Womankind, a women and mental health project based in Bristol

Henderson Hospital: Greater than the sum of its sub-groups

Dr Kingsley Norton[1]

Mental health workers and service users inhabit a world of groups and sub-groups. They navigate this universe largely unconsciously, usually without reflection. As a result, it is possible to ignore or minimize the importance of the group settings in which they work, including influences that promote or hinder healthy psychological and social functioning.

The democratic therapeutic community (TC) is a deliberate attempt to structure a setting that can recognise the totality of the institution (without losing sight of the individual) and to establish processes to confront un-integrated constituent elements. Its aim is to promote personality maturation via the creation of a culture that values participation in both formal therapy groups and the informal social times in between. The TC relies on the positive contribution of its service users and requires staff to delegate to them much of the power and authority traditionally invested in their roles. Thereby it aims to access healthy influences not usually available, through interaction, exploration and experimentation and to diminish destructive coping styles and strategies.

This paper describes the workings of Henderson Hospital's TC, outlining its structure and, importantly, the ideological 'culture' in which the work is undertaken. The treatment programme is described in relation to the diverse needs of the service users.

'Community' is where everyone knows your name and someone notices when you're not there. (Chief Rabbi, Jonathan Sacks; 'Thought for the day', Radio 4, 2001)

Key words: *therapeutic community; personality disorder; group participation*

Introduction

Henderson is a National Health Service Hospital based in Sutton, Surrey. The hospital is run as a democratic therapeutic community (TC) for up to 29 clients suffering from severe personality disorder. The notion of 'community' implies a high degree of harmonisation of its constituent parts - an integrated whole. At a concrete level, a TC is often a single entity, clearly identifiable by virtue of having its own front door and address or having its own building and grounds. Yet, at the level of internal relationships and structures, it may not be obvious how deep such singularity goes. Indeed, it is possible that scratching the surface of a TC will reveal inconsistencies and contradictions. This is why the notion of wholeness may be more apparent than real, more of an ideal to be striven for than an everyday reality. However, in as much as the whole does not operate in an integrated manner, the full potential of a TC to be 'therapeutic' may not be realised. Indeed, for much of the time, it is as if Henderson's clients themselves desire to atomise the TC - for it to become a set of meaningless, inhuman structures. Staff too can play a destructive role. This paper attempts to address the issue of how the parts of Henderson's TC relate to its whole. By becoming whole, the Henderson TC provides a flexible alignment of its personal, interpersonal and social systems and thereby maximises its therapeutic potential. The fictitious case described below gives an indication of Henderson's clientele.

Client example
B is a 28 year old unemployed single woman whose two children were adopted shortly after birth.

B had been admitted to the local acute psychiatric ward from the Accident and Emergency Department. She had slashed both her wrists following a row with her ex-boyfriend. This was the latest in a long series of violent relationships with men. None lasted more than a few months. B had become pregnant on five occasions but only two of these had gone to term. On both occasions the infant had been removed into care to be adopted shortly afterwards, as B was not considered by the authorities to be a fit mother.

B herself had been the product of a short-lived relationship. Her mother had many partners subsequently, some of whom had sexually abused B. It was not clear whether mother had been aware of this as B was growing up. The latter had been noted to be intelligent when assessed at primary school but had played truant from an early age and been expelled for violence to a teacher when at secondary school. By this time she was already abusing both alcohol and 'soft' drugs. This behaviour escalated after leaving school to include heroin addiction. To feed this habit B had prostituted herself on a number of occasions. She was now positive for Hepatitis B.

At interview on the psychiatric ward, B was noted to have multiple scars on both arms and some on her abdomen. She described herself as feeling 'empty and dead inside'- feelings that were relieved in the short-term by her self-harming. She intermittently heard 'a male voice' inside her head but there was no evidence of a major mood disorder or of psychosis. On the ward she quickly settled into the routine not appearing unduly depressed. She made friends with the younger patients there and was continually asking favours of the younger staff members, sometimes being intrusive and sexually inappropriate. She left the ward on her third day and returned with cannabis, which she encouraged other patients to share. She was discharged on account of this after it was discovered since there were no reasons to consider compulsory detention. She has been treated via the local day hospital and had a range of psychological treatments and day treatment. None have provided lasting improvements.

Personality disorder

The psychiatric description of Personality Disorder (PD) suggests that 'the pattern is stable and of long duration and its onset can be tracked back at least to adolescence or early childhood'. In addition, 'the enduring pattern is inflexible and pervasive across a broad range of personal and social situations'. (American Psychiatric Association, 1994, p 633).

Clearly, the relationships these people form are frequently stressful and often destructive, as in the case of B. When it comes to organising therapeutic help for them it is well to remember that their difficulties may arise at all levels of human relationships: personal, interpersonal and social. This range and diversity of problematic contexts is a complicating factor for any organisation setting itself up to offer help to this client group. A delicate balance therefore needs to be struck between being intrusive or interventionist and unduly permissive or 'laissez faire'. The former is experienced by clients as abusive and the latter as neglectful. As such, each extreme feels like the continuation or repeat of earlier traumatization. These experiences offer no new models of relationship that clients could emulate or internalise.

One way of tackling the complexity deriving from the client's spread of personal, interpersonal and social problems is to search for themes that connect these domains. On close examination, some connecting threads emerge. These are reflected in patterns of thinking, feeling, relating and behaving. Many with PD, especially antisocial PD, are said not to learn from experience. Hence their behaviour may remain deviant (compared to social and cultural norms) even in spite of social censure, fines or imprisonment. However, much of the client's experiences are such as to have taught extreme, often self-destructive or outwardly violent, coping strategies or defence mechanisms. At the time of early abusive or neglecting relationships such manoeuvres may have been literally life-saving to the individual. In later life, however, this continuing pattern tends not to serve as well, since they confer a rigid set of behaviours that do not sufficiently mirror the demands of a more or less equal interpersonal relationship, such as is required in a mutually enhancing, adult partnership.

The client's relationships may however be stably unstable, with a clear pattern of dominance-submission or independence-dependence, though this may vary according to the relationship domain. For example, one partner is dominant in the sexual arena but submissive in major decision-making about domestic matters. Because the relationship may be stable and the interpersonal coping strategies deeply ingrained it may be difficult for clients to give up their usual roles and behaviours. Little learning from recent experience occurs spontaneously i.e. without a therapeutic input.

Facing the potential of a different, non-traumatizing, relationship, as in the context of therapy, therefore poses as much of a problem as it does a solution to such clients. Consciously and unconsciously, therefore, they may undermine attempts made by a therapist (see later) to understand links between their behaviour and feelings or thoughts, in the service of avoiding suffering in the short-term. This taxes and challenges the skills and patience of the professional. It can be hard for a single therapist to withstand the provocation to over- or under-invest in the professional relationship with some PD clients. The professional is often 'set up' to fail since they will not be able to satisfy the client – at least in the short term. Dealing with personal frustration can be difficult to manage in isolation and therapeutic failure may result. It is often therefore that a team approach is required, hence the need for partial or complete hospitalisation to withstand such attacks.

Many clients 'act' rather than thinking or feeling to minimize the psychological pain. This frequently appears as impulsivity (see later). To the onlooker, including sometimes the therapist, such action may be inappropriate to the situation and apparently irrational. In as much as it is out of consciousness, the client him/herself may also be caught unawares, as in the case of a young woman who was only aware of her 'deliberate' self-harming once embarked on the cutting itself. She came to herself in the act of self-mutilation. Such behaviour is difficult to manage in out-patient settings and in isolation, hence the need for multi-disciplinary/multi-agency collaboration and sometimes residential treatment, as at Henderson Hospital.

Endings or the threat of endings of relationships, can often be sufficient to provoke impulsive self-damaging or other destructive behaviour. This is because of a fear of this representing a total abandonment, as if the client will never regain any contact with another. The relationships in question, some of which may be of only short duration, are nevertheless imbued with personal significance for the client. It can occur in relation to a professional carrying out an assessment interview for treatment. As mentioned above, some relationships, especially where the client's partner shares similar or complementary personality traits, can be stably unstable. In such a situation the relationship is marked by reciprocal approaching-distancing and each role elicits a complementary response, often associated with impulsive behaviour at each threatened 'abandonment'. This pattern frequently recapitulates that of earlier traumatizing relationships in childhood, not only supporting its continuation but causing little potential for change and for the development of a more coherent sense of self. What is required is an environment that can both withstand their re-enactment and also provide space both for exploration (of causes and effects) and also experimentation with other coping strategies (Whiteley, 1986).

The therapeutic community is designed to provide such a facilitating environment (Winnicott, 1965). Where the person's difficulties may surface at all levels of relationship, then a whole system in which all the levels are available for learning is helpful. Yet, it is necessary to ensure that the experiences lead to learning rather than provide more opportunities for acting out or avoidance. The learning comes into it when the real difficulties are identified with each person and new strategies of dealing with each are learned. To ensure that information constantly flows quickly and accurately from one level to another, channels of communication about each and every experience have to be developed and kept constantly open. This requirement is the reason for developing a sophisticated system of communication that encompasses all possible experiences around the clock – day and night, seven days a week. Such a degree of efficiency can evolve only within a single system that is seen by all to be a whole – a web of sub-groups, all interwoven into a totality that ensures clear and meaningful communication among all its parts. Such an ideal 'holistic' stance characterises the concept of the TC that will be explained now.

The concept of therapeutic community

It was Tom Main who suggested the term 'therapeutic community' in his seminal paper 'The hospital as a therapeutic institution' (Main, 1946). Later, he coined the phrase 'culture of enquiry' to refer to the crucial feature of the therapeutic community (Main, 1983). In his view it was this self-conscious scrutiny of the institution and its inhabitants by the institution itself that distinguished it from other psychiatric enterprises. Creating and sustaining a culture that is conducive to such an enquiry is a complex task, more than merely setting up certain structures, such as community and small psychotherapy group meetings.

Another pioneer of the approach, Maxwell Jones, conceived of the therapeutic community (TC) in a broadly similar way to Main, but emphasised far more strongly the use of many different types of groupwork (Jones, 1952). Jones realised that a restructuring of the traditional hierarchies among staff and between staff and patients was also needed. The culture he developed at the Henderson, from 1947, provided deeper collaboration around tasks shared among the different disciplines within the multidisciplinary team. His was a 'living-learning' environment. Achieving this was necessary though difficult and it posed a challenge to traditional methods, which tended to underestimate the impact of the social environment (including that of the professionals involved), not only as part of the cause of mental ill-health, but also as part of its treatment. For Jones, the reorganisation included more open communication; less rigid hierarchy; and daily discussions of the whole unit and its sub-groups.

The ideas and practices of both Main and Jones represented the addition of a 'systems' way of conceiving the psychiatric environment (von Bertalannfy, 1967). To an extent, therefore, the TC represents the application, and potential integration, of different theoretical frameworks, including that of group analysis, more or less simultaneously (Norton and Haigh, 2001) The notion of the person as simply a biomedical entity was rejected (Gray et al. 1969). Not only was there a psychological dimension to the individual but also a social dimension. People inhabiting a psychiatric ward are thus simultaneously members of various interacting 'systems', all of which have their particular aims, methods and outputs. With this plurality and richness, however, comes the potential for ideological clashes and for contradictory goals, reflecting different sub-systems within the TC, especially the patient and staff sub-systems.

Various functions, such as patients' involvement, containment and support can be offered within various structures. Yet, only when these functions are integrated into a whole is the 'therapeutic community proper' (Clarke, 1965) created. This means that there needs to be selection of clients, that the TC is not suitable for all, and that a rich timetable of therapeutic activities is needed to address the varying needs of the client group involved.

Implication for practice

Maintaining an integrated TC 'supra-system' is inherently problematic. The difficulty is compounded when the community comprises individuals with different capacities and motivations. This is the more so when some participants are psychologically disordered and ambivalent about being in that situation at all. This is the case for the democratic TC at Henderson. It is now deployed in the treatment of those suffering from personality disorder. They are notoriously difficult to treat regardless of treatment modality (Norton and Hinshelwood, 1996). It is crucial, therefore, that there is an understanding of the basic issues and themes already mentioned. The goal of the therapeutic endeavour is to facilitate 'actors and non-feelers' to become 'thinkers and feelers' (Norton, 1992). This needs to be clearly stated and understood, ideally by all concerned. However, this is only ever the first step, since the test of the method is how it deals with the actual interaction between the system of the TC and its sub-systems, especially the sub-systems of the staff and the clients.

The primary task is to manage safely the inevitable interpersonal turbulence. These tensions especially emanate from the clients' internal conflicts being enacted. Upheavals have to be managed within safe limits. While these are maintained, it is necessary to maximise the therapeutic potential which requires the clients to experience a different style of relating, as well as participate in an enquiring culture to which they are not used (Gabbard, 1988; Norton and Dolan, 1995). Faced with the unfamiliar, there is often at least an unconscious drive to repeat our past relationships. So, in the TC, there is a drive for the abuses and neglect that clients experienced in the past to become repeated in the present - with the staff or fellow clients and frequently with both. The potential 'new' relationships, those that attempt to avoid this predictable outcome, are mistrusted and consequently tested for their genuineness - repeatedly. This is why managing countertransferential reactions is an on-going issue and process for the staff team. They require support and supervision to maintain adequately this important function.

In the democratic TC, the client is expected to be responsible for two major areas: (1) abiding by the rules of the community- a microcosm of those obtaining in outside society, and (2) participating in the daily running of the unit, i.e. taking a turn in the administrative, practical and therapeutic tasks, according to seniority in the treatment programme. Therefore, the selection process (effected by staff and clients but with a client majority and on the basis of a democratic vote) is there to ascertain, as far as is possible, that the clients selected have the necessary attributes to succeed (Dolan et al. 1990).

At the selection interview, the candidates are apprised of the requirements for membership. Following selection, turning up for admission is taken as an agreement, no matter how ambivalent, to accept the terms and conditions described above. Of course, from then on, clients struggle with their tendency to avoid change by clashing with the authority structures or the reverse, playing by the rules in the hope that this will magically result in benefit accruing (Norton, 1996). However, whether clients 'act out' or otherwise 'avoid' change, there are community mechanisms to deal with these eventualities, through a mix of challenge and support. In broad terms, these are illustrated in the diagram below (Norton & Warren, in press).

Some clients, whose tendency is to 'act out' their internal conflict, will cycle around the left-hand circuit in excess of twenty times in the course of the maximum stay of one year. This represents the repeated breaking of the major rules of the TC (i.e. no violence to self, others or property) or transgression of rules prohibiting consumption of alcohol and illicit use of drugs. However, the culture includes also a limited degree of tolerance of acting out. Some degree of such 'misbehaviour' is therefore accepted, provided that a client is seen by their peers and staff to be struggling seriously to abide by the rules and to be using available 'groups' to explore their difficulties and appropriately draw on other clients for support.

Those who predominantly 'avoid' change may be harder to detect. These clients will take longer to encounter the mechanism that is there to challenge what is often a subtle defence - that of the 'perfect' or 'model' client. Their 'career' in the TC is depicted at the right hand circuit. Characteristically, they will have been helpful to the community in practical ways, even showing themselves to be reliable in giving support to others. What will not have been evinced, however, is any meaningful emotional engagement with others. They will not have been able to take emotionally from others. Clients seldom traverse this route more than once since, as soon as their coping strategy is exposed, a great deal of pressure is exerted by the peer group for change. Disappointment, anger and rejection, are strongly expressed if there is none forthcoming. The only sanction then is discharge with readmission impossible, at least not within six months.

Whatever the strategy for avoiding authentic change, all clients share one need. This need is to have their strengths recognised in whatever form these take, while their weaknesses are pointed out. To this end the therapeutic programme has aspects that represent non-verbal as well as verbal aspects, providing the potential to reveal areas of relative strength or competence from as wide a range of settings and activities as possible. Crucially, the time between the formal sessions of therapy is conceived as equally part of the total programme (Whiteley and Collis, 1987). This is the time during which many of the everyday tasks required for the smooth-running of the community (e.g. ordering, storing and cooking of the food for the TC) will be undertaken (or not) as part of the performing of 'jobs' to which clients are elected by their peers on a monthly basis. Giving and receiving feedback on how clients perform these roles becomes an important part of therapy.

As a consequence, therapy is not simply about the past but also about present functioning. Beginning to develop a feeling of

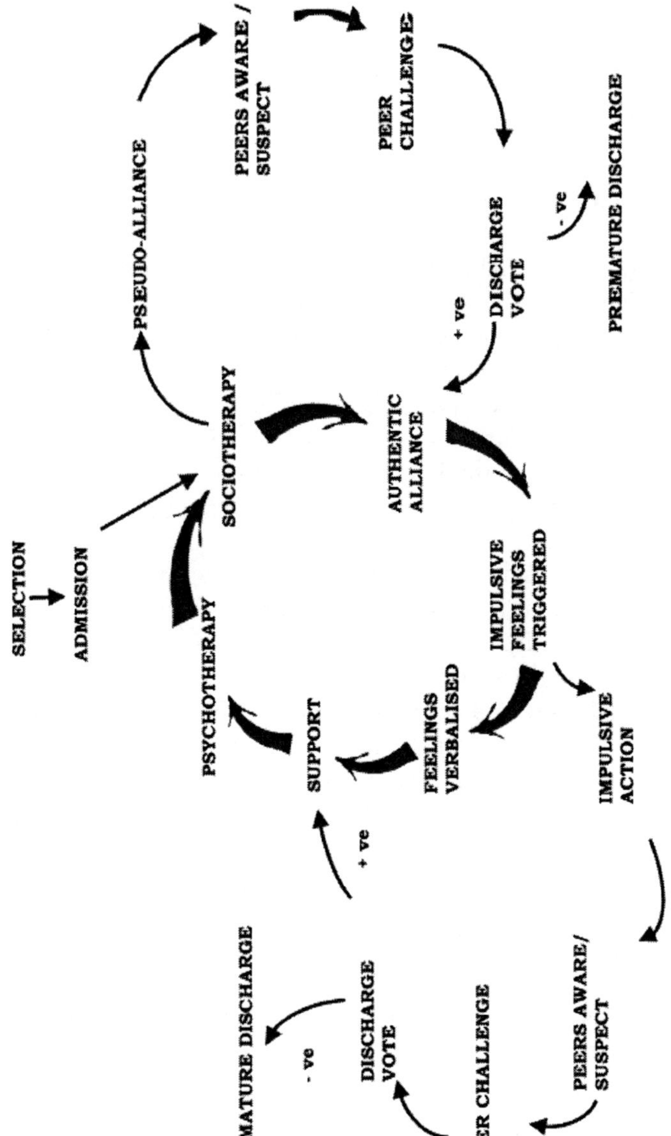

Figure 1: In-patient sociotherapeutic and psychotherapeutic processes

belonging to the community, through participating in the 'give and take' of communal life, is to many a novel experience. Increasingly this is felt by clients as a privilege that could be lost. On this basis, it is the clients themselves who are the 'culture carriers' and who exert the greatest 'corrective' influence on the rest of the client group (Mahony, 1979).

Organizing the day

The range of activities shown below (Table 1) is organized so as to provide a predictable set of experiences, which enable both staff and clients to anticipate what is due to happen next as far as this is possible. This predictability is so important to those whose previous lives and experiences have lacked order. It represents an important aspect of 'structure' (Gunderson, 1978). Beyond this, however, the shared nature of the knowledge about the treatment programme fosters a levelling of the traditional staff- client hierarchy, wherein only the staff know what's going on and what to expect during a given day. Clients are expected to be in certain places at certain times and so it is necessary to monitor attendance, to observe if what is intended actually happens.

There is therefore a mechanism, involving both the clients and staff, to record accurately whether clients attend as planned. There is also a mechanism that allows clients to miss a scheduled activity, with prior permission having been granted. In this way they can be confronted with consequences of their behaviour, resulting from the extent to which they do what they say they will do. This includes receiving feedback from staff, but particularly from their peer group, on any upset which may have resulted from non-attendance or breaking of trust through the clients' actions not marrying up with their words.

Here are brief descriptions about each of the group meetings that clients attend.

Community meeting

Most of the confronting of patients with their failure to attend any

Table 1: Weekly programme

TABLE 1-WEEKLY PROGRAMME

Time	MONDAY	TUESDAY	WEDNESDAY Groups	THURSDAY	FRIDAY	SATURDAY	SUNDAY
9.15 – 10.30 a.m.		*"9.15" Community Meeting*					
10.30 a.m.		Morning Break					
	Small Groups / *New Residents' Group* 11.00 – 12.00 noon	*Cleaning & Reviews or Elections or Community Projects* 11.00 – 12.00 noon	*Small group Residents' Group Leavers' Group Transition* 10.30 – 11.30 a.m.	*New Visitors' Group Women's Group Men's Group* 11.00 – 12.00 noon	*Small Groups New Residents' Group* 11.00 – 12.00 noon		
12.15 – 12.30		CLEANING					
12.30		LUNCH BREAK					
Surgery 1.00 –1.30 p.m. Floor Reps meeting 1.30 - 1.45 p.m. Sports & Social 1.45 – 2.10 p.m.		Surgery 2.05 – 2.15 p.m.	Surgery 2.05 – 2.15 p.m. GLO Meeting 12.30 – 12.50 p.m.	Surgery 2.05 – 2.15 p.m.	Surgery 2.05 – 2.15 p.m.		
2.30 – 4.15 p.m.	*Psychodrama or Art Therapy* 2.30 – 4.15 p.m.	*Selection/Unit Reception or Welfare or Sports and Social* 2.30 – 4.15 p.m.	*Psychodrama or Art Therapy* 2.30 – 4.15 p.m.	*Work Groups (Art or Gardening Maintenance)* 2.15 – 4.15 p.m.	*Work Groups (Art, Welfare or Gardening Maintenance)* 2.15 – 4.15 p.m. Tea 4.30 – 5.00 p.m.		
5.00 p.m.		HANDOVER					
7.00 – 9.00 p.m.		COMMUNITY MEAL					
9.45 - 10.30 p.m.		SUMMIT MEETING (Top 4 Residents and staff)				9.45 - 10.30 p.m. Summit	10.05 P.M. Summit Booking in
11.00 p.m.		NIGHT ROUND					

Weekdays
Welfare Phone Slot
10.30 a.m. – 11.00 a.m.
12.30 p.m. – 1.00 p.m.

* Visitors' Day (Professional visitors) - Thursday 8.45 a.m. - 5.00 p.m.
Community Afternoon - last Thursday in month 2.15 p.m. - 4.15 p.m. (NB Those group meetings referred to in the text are denoted in italics).

of the group meetings of the programme is carried out in a meeting of the entire community, i.e. all clients and those staff on duty on a given day. This meeting has an agenda and is chaired by one of the senior clients, elected to one of three -' Top Three' - positions for a month at a time. The meetings take place every day (except Sundays) at the same time- 9.15am Most days' agendas are basically similar but with differences that reflect:

1. what is to follow that day, in as much as this is distinctive and
2. what from the previous day and night needs to be processed and assimilated.

This enables the community, the individuals comprising it, to learn from experience - 'living-learning'- something which a personality disordered client group is said to have difficulties in doing. More specifically, during this meeting the dynamics of large groups tend to emerge. In the long run, understanding and learning to deal with such dynamics can be helpful to clients in many work and social situations later on outside.

A specimen agenda is provided below to give an impression of the amount of daily business that the community generates and to offer a sense of the level of responsibility taken by the elected senior clients who in turn chair it, during their 4 weeks tenure of office. Implicit is the authority delegated by staff to the meeting. This represents the giving up of a significant amount of traditionally held staff power.

Emergency meeting

Having elaborated some of the regular and predictable time-structuring, it is now important to describe how this can be overridden by an emergency ('referred') meeting, which can be called at any time of the day or night by the Top Three residents in collaboration with the two ' duty staff'. The latter, who stand in for the whole staff team during the 9-5, Monday to Friday, are the only staff present in the community at all other times- 76 per cent of the entire week. It is this group of 5 – staff and residents - who decide how to respond in the face of an unexpected or untoward event or issue.

Typical Community Meeting Agenda

'Good morning'		
Who's missing?	=	Resident (or assistant) to report absentees
Handover (rota'd clients)	=	Residents to take part in 5 p.m. handover to staff
Wash-ups (rota'd clients)	=	Lunch, tea, supper (daily)
Supper	=	Cooks - volunteers
Staff feedback	=	staff absence (leave, sickness etc.), other staff movements, issues not otherwise covered on Agenda
'Referred' and yesterday's feedback	=	Emergency meetings, and unstructured time fed back
Groups' feedback	=	Previous day's groups fed back
'Summit Discussed'	=	Summit meeting topics fed back to rest of community
'Groups, votes, and why?'	=	Report on those who missed groups or broke major rules
Ask for S.I.E.s	=	Those technically discharged by rule breaking seek temporary re-instatement
['Votes' taken]		
Emergency extensions	=	Asking permission to absent group(s)
'Meeting closed'		

Their first task is to establish the urgency of the situation. Having judged a given situation to be urgent, the next step is to call a 'referred meeting', usually within 15 minutes of having made the decision to do so. In addition to risk assessment and measurement, this meeting serves a reflective functioning, which represents an important modelling of responding thoughtfully, as opposed to automatically, i.e. simply according to a past judgement of apparently similar events or issues. Many clients will have an underdeveloped capacity to evaluate situations (or indeed their own self-states) under conditions of stress. As a result, they may rate everything as equally 'urgent' and act accordingly - with an expectation that others will necessarily concur and support. Failure in the past by others, including previous staff involved with them, to share their sense of priorities may have contributed to difficulties with treatment alliance and to the breakdown of the professional relationship.

In these referred meetings, which are also chaired by one of the Top Three, the issue in question is presented to the whole community for its thoughts and for any necessary decisions and action. As stated, they can be called at any time and they take priority over all other activity, including any of the formal treatment ingredients. All clients on the Unit are expected to attend and as many of the staff as possible but always the two 'duty staff', who were also party to the decision to call the meeting. It is in this forum that all the important decisions are made, for example, the premature discharge of clients, via the taking of a democratic vote. (Clients' numbers always outweigh those of staff, aiding the authenticity of their empowerment). Learning to cope with the confusing mix of feelings associated with 'crisis' is part of the process of increasing reflection and decreasing impulsive action (see below). Experiencing crisis, confusion and uncertainty and learning new skills with which to cope is expected to be helpful to clients in their relationships outside too – be they personal, interpersonal or even social.

Small psychotherapy groups

Three times per week there are small group psychotherapy meetings, each facilitated by up to three staff members. These groups, which contain approximately seven or eight clients, allow an exploration of both past and recent events. Insights gained from these groups can feed a cautious experimentation with new coping strategies (Whiteley, 1986). This leads to new ways of coping that can be re-explored and then brought back to the forum of the small group. In this way a cycle of interaction, exploration and experimentation can be repeatedly set up, with beneficial results. Many of this client group lack a well-developed capacity to verbalise their distress and difficulties. Therefore, enactment of emotional and interpersonal conflicts is desirable - provided this can be offered within a safe-enough setting. The capacity to connect action and reaction without these being made explicit is needed if clients are to engage in close friendships and intimate relationships outside.

Work groups

In order for the usual strategies, and more importantly interpersonal difficulties, to be re-encountered there is as much of everyday reality as safely possible within the therapeutic community. As part of this there are non-verbal groups, which serve a number of purposes. They give those with non-verbal skills a chance to shine and those who 'talk the talk', but cannot quite 'walk the walk', opportunities to display their difficulties with everyday problems, such as being unable to work with others or to complete a concrete task. All of this, whether success or failure, is grist to the community's psycho- and socio-therapeutic mill.

This is the case provided that the opportunities for exploration and experimentation are seized. In practice, most clients are reticent to expose their vulnerabilities. It takes senior clients, leading by example, to induce sufficient confidence or courage in newer clients, as in Jones' seminal observation that it was those clients senior in the psycho-educational programme he was running who were best at inducting new clients and explaining to them what was the intended message, i.e. he saw that clients were, in many respects, superior teachers to the trained staff. The lessons drawn are expected to stand them in good stead when clients enter work or further education outside.

Jobs

Ideally, all the clients in the TC will participate in its daily working. There are many tasks to undertake, which in a more traditional setting would be carried out by staff, particularly nursing and medical. Some of these are delegated to clients to do alone and others in collaboration with peers or staff themselves. These include important administrative aspects such as the chairing of: community meetings; 'referred' (emergency) meetings; and selection interviews for acceptance into the community (see above). The recording of content at certain meetings, namely 'referred' and 'selection' (see timetable), is also delegated to the clients, although, a record is kept independently by staff. It is the client's record that is used as part of the business of the community, in the sense of being read out in the community meeting – another job to be done. The ordering of food, within an agreed budget, its storage and preparation for the meals are all led by the residents but with staff collaboration in the actual negotiation with the wider world outside. Importantly, this means that if insufficient food or inappropriate food is ordered it is the community who suffer the consequences and it will often be the responsible clients who are called to account – 'reality confrontation' (Rapoport, 1960).

Although all jobs need to be done, some are inevitably more important than others and these are reserved for the more senior clients, in practice, those who have been in treatment for at least three months. In effect they will have served an apprenticeship for most jobs, from having worked in an assistant capacity while more junior in the community. Clients can nominate themselves or be nominated to a particular post at the monthly 'elections'. This meeting, which is also chaired by one of the 'Top Three', will attempt to fill all the posts since all fall vacant at the same time. This maximises the chance that everybody will have an opportunity to perform all the roles within the community during the year of their stay. It also makes it less likely that only certain personalities will dominate the principal organising roles, since this would be conspicuous and obvious to all concerned and could be challenged. While staff may comment on nominations, or indeed nominate, they do not have a vote in the appointment to any post. This means that the client sub-system is empowered and thereby in a stronger position to learn from the experience of their own decisions and choices- for better or worse.

Unstructured time

Many clients, especially those who are familiar with prison culture, appear to believe that it will be sufficient to merely abide by the rules of the therapeutic community and attend all groups – 'to keep their noses clean' – for them to derive benefit. Such clients may be popular, at least initially, since they often become the 'model' patients referred to earlier, eager to help others, especially with the more concrete and manual tasks. It may take some months before this coping strategy or defence is seen for what it is and, even then, it may be difficult to challenge successfully (see above). Individuals utilising such a survival strategy seldom have many other resources on which to draw.

However, since part of the unwritten contract is to participate actively, non-participation in any aspect of the programme becomes a potential reason for discharge. Participation does therefore include the use of free time, because this time is also an opportunity to reveal the person's more human side - including a measure of vulnerability. This is why the informal time is also part of therapy and what goes on during these hours, whether or not the activity is useful to the individual or the community, is legitimately open for discussion and challenge.

Many clients find it difficult to structure for themselves the time which is free at the weekends - from mid-morning on Saturday till late Sunday evening. It is tempting then to resort to usual coping mechanisms, such as self-mutilation, getting drunk, taking drugs or indulging in violence to others. Clearly the capacity of the community to 'police' itself is limited and reliance is placed on honesty. Initially, this is hoped for rather than expected. Acquiring a capacity to structure time is expected to help clients with real friendships and family relations outside too.

The timetable outlined above thus needs to be conceived more as an organic 'whole' than as a shopping-list of necessary group meetings.

Addressing psychological processes

Through their participation in democratic processes and their deep level of involvement in the daily running of the community, the client sub-system has exerted a profound influence on the development of the programme of groups. This approach is thus more or less tailor-made to their requirements - at least in theory (Norton, 1992). With no individual therapy offered, group structures, in combination, enable the solution of the difficulties that are presented and experienced by this population. These difficulties are distinguished thematically (as discussed above) and used below to create sub-sections of this paper. They suggest how the programme and the unstructured time, separately, combine with one another and relate to the clients' habitual personal and interpersonal difficulties. The latter are identified, as follows:

- identity diffusion (Erikson, 1956);
- attacks on linking (Bion, 1961);
- impulsivity (Kernberg, 1966); *and*
- abandonment fears (Masterson, 1972).

Identity diffusion: Meeting emergencies

Typically, Henderson clients oscillate between a 'whirlwind mentality' and being 'becalmed' (Norton, 1997). It is this that can often induce a similar pattern of reacting in staff who either panic or feel paralysed and defeated. As above, such 'complementary' responses by staff and others remove the potential for thinking and reacting afresh in the future (Norton and Dolan, 1995). Clients thus continue in not knowing truly how they stand in relation to others and, as importantly, how they stand in relation to themselves. They have an 'identity diffusion', i.e. a poorly integrated concept of self and of significant others (Kernberg, 1984).

One of the trademarks of the democratic TC developed at Henderson Hospital is its capacity to respond to individual upset or interpersonal discord with speed. In this respect it is not essentially different from any acute psychiatric ward or locked environment. However, what is distinctive is the fact that, in effect, the whole treatment team is available straight away. Thus the full decision-making, risk assessment and management apparatus, for each of the 24 hours of the day, is always present. Responses to the upset or discord are organised through the emergency or 'referred' meeting. Regardless of the time, anything from 'informal support' to 'discharge' can be organised, depending on the situation and taking account of the level of risk involved. This contrasts starkly with the more traditional psychiatric ward situation, especially at night. There it is imperative to close down any untoward event as speedily as possible and involve as few as possible of the patients in it. Often the relevant personnel for making important clinical decisions are absent and decisions that are made are in relation to short-term management only. The opposite obtains in the democratic TC.

During the emergency meeting (see above), after whatever risk-reducing emergency measures have been put in place, there will be an examination of the people and issues that prompted it. The attempt is to explore both the antecedents and consequences of the disturbance, including what action, if any, the community should now take in relation to a given client. This forum provides clients with a powerful experience of the immediate consequences of their attitudes and behaviours, which are 'past their sell by dates', in terms of having useful survival value. Such exploration occurs close to the event and with a high level of expressive freedom on the part of the client peer group. Therefore, it provides a greater learning potential than if feedback were received later, for example, from staff at a weekly ward round, or multidisciplinary team meeting, or even the next group meeting in the formal programme of the TC.

Extreme patterns of behaving and relating (such as self-harming), which have been habitual are now reinterpreted (and re-experienced), often as shocking and unacceptable. Through being responded to in an authentic but, ultimately, non-extreme and non-complementary way, simple condoning or condemnation (as well as over-reacting or ignoring) are avoided. Mixed in with this implicit challenge - to develop other, more adaptive (less aggressive or passive-aggressive), means of communicating distress - is much support and empathy. The latter is available since many of those challenging will have analogous, similar or even identical self-destructive or self-defeating patterns of behaving.

This experience contrasts markedly both with the responses of familiar others and of professionals who, after years of stalemate, are often left feeling defeated or frustrated and unable to offer anything new. The benefit of the TC experience for the client is the achievement of a clearer sense of self and other, through inhabiting an environment that reflects back to them a more complex and integrated – less diffuse- view of themselves. In this sense it validates them (Gunderson, 1978). This situation also obtains in relation to the learning potential of the so-called 'work groups', psychodrama, art therapy and welfare groups, which all have an after-group, strategically placed, so that what has just happened can be examined while it is still fresh in everybody's mind.

Attacks on linking: Integration of groups

There is a universal tendency in us all to cling to what is known and to ignore contrary evidence to that which we believe to be true. We often fail to identify therefore what is 'new' and to integrate this material, hence learn from experience and change. The clients of the Henderson exemplify this tendency particularly clearly. Not least this is because of the extremeness of much of their past experience, whether of neglect or abuse. As a result there is sometimes an unconscious but sometimes a deliberate attempt to uncouple an understanding of any linkage between the past and the present. Therefore there is frequently a drive to pervert various aspects of the TC structure, so as to avoid encountering what is novel and reflecting on its personal and emotional significance. Thus life remains meaningless, with emotional aspects uncoupled from life's events. Three examples of this may illustrate the point.

First, as described above, the agenda of the daily community meeting is modified at a small group meeting the previous evening – called 'Summit'. At this meeting are the two night staff and four senior clients, elected to fulfil this role. The latter are the 'Top Three' and 'General Secretary'. One task for the Summit is to review the whole of the previous 24 hours and to adjust the agenda of the next day's meeting in accordance with that. This is so as to attend to whatever TC business is practically relevant and psychologically pressing. The job of the General Secretary is to write out the whole agenda for the next day's community meeting. Ostensibly, the task is straightforward.

However, given the circumstances and the high level of anxiety that often accompanies them, the work is not so easy to achieve. The clients may wish to obtain 'therapy' from the two night staff for themselves (i.e. not reviewing the 'whole'), having given so much to others for the last day. Spurious items may be discussed in place of more pertinent issues, and this is sometimes difficult to spot because of a clever camouflage. Sometimes there may be silence or at least passivity, out of a belief that the staff are the true experts and, in any case, are being paid to do their jobs. All of these, and many more avoidant tactics, stand in the way of a smooth pursuit of task during the 'Summit' meeting.

Second, the following morning, it is customary that what is written down, as having been discussed at 'Summit', is separately reported by the Chair to the next day's community meeting. However, this report may bear little or no resemblance to what was actually discussed. Consequently, the meaning of the item on the next day's agenda, which relates to feedback from the previous evening's Summit to the rest of the community, is at risk of being perverted i.e. there is an attack on a 'past-present' linkage. Such an attack can take many forms: what was discussed is summarised cryptically and without expansion in spite of requests for clarification; something not discussed but merely mentioned in passing may be presented; the chairing client allows any ensuing discussion to wander from the originally presented matters. There are more potential manoeuvrings at each stage, i.e. at both summit and community meeting feedback, all of which serve to dislocate the events and emotional issues of yesterday from the psychological business of today and block thinking about, hence learning from, past experience. Staff may need to work hard to bring in the avoided material, often strongly affective in type as in this third example.

Third, in the 'transition group', when it was newly established, news of just what it felt like to have left the TC was fed back by ex-clients to those senior clients preparing to leave. It was often painful and thus difficult to hear. Formal feedback from this group was repeatedly absent from the agenda of the community meeting, as if there were a client sub-system denial of the painful reality of leaving. No linkage took place. It took some time for staff to appreciate and comment upon the absence of feedback from this important group but eventually this occurred with benefit and the community was sensitised to this particular avoidant tactic, at least for at time.

Contributing to problems with linking, staff may not feel confident to challenge the client 'chair' of this large group meeting, usually around forty in number. If they do, as did happen in the instances described above, what often ensues is dispute between client and staff sub-systems. Sometimes the argument itself successfully distracts from what should have been discussed, thus maintaining an absence of the linking of emotional material to events. In the third instance described above, it was sadness and anger surrounding the important issues of leaving and loss. Finding creative ways of bringing avoided material into the community meeting is a challenge to the collective staff skills. In part, success in this venture rests on the ability of the staff system to identify 'basic assumption' functioning (Bion, 1961; see also Roberts, 1980) and to spot when the primary task associated with the meeting's agenda item is avoided or adulterated.

Impulsivity: Planned action and play

Many of the Henderson clients often inhabit a timeless world dominated by impulse and unrealistic expectations of self and others. Time rushes or else stands still (Norton, 1997b). Omnipotent or impotent fantasies, some unconscious and others conscious, influence their interactions with others. These extreme fluctuations make encounters with therapists likely to fail because of the difficulty of sharing a stable and realistic treatment alliance or 'contract' (Miller, 1989). This detracts from a cohesive self that could draw on a past and anticipate a future. The challenge is to sustain a 'present', a reflective transitional 'space' (Winnicott, 1968) in which can be found a capacity to evaluate and judge – to think thoughts (Bion, 1961). Together, many of the treatment programme ingredients and their daily and weekly structuring, contribute to the installation of a more realistic sense of time, place and person, i.e. higher levels of ego functioning. Such progress ensures less diffuse identity and decreased likelihood of 'acting out' of internal conflict. Psychodrama is perhaps best-placed among these treatment ingredients to focus on events with the potential for safe experimentation with 'alternative' pasts, presents and futures. Of course, the results of such experimentation, for protagonists and audience, become the stuff of further exploration in small psychotherapy groups.

It is important that the TC is so structured that the clients meet with as much of outside life - 'social reality' - as possible (Main, 1946). Without this, clients will not encounter the usual triggers to their impulsive and self-destructive or maladaptive behaviours and neither staff nor peers will see adequately what the problem is. This is because ordinary verbal communication skills tend to be lacking for these clients - being either underdeveloped or under-used, when it comes to clarifying and conveying emotional or interpersonal conflict (Norton, 1997a). For the TC situation to be therapeutic and also safe, the first or early behavioural signs of personal upset or interpersonal discord need to be observed. In the TC, with its emphasis on the whole 24 hours and not just the formal therapy programme, there is more time and personnel (because of the active participation of clients) to accomplish this observational task than in the traditional psychiatric ward environment. It is thus unlikely that much impulsive, destructive activity goes on without somebody knowing about, or at least suspecting, it.

Observation is only the first step, however. Information needs to be communicated either to one of the smaller group meetings or to the whole community. (Often this is effected via an emergency meeting). It has already been stressed how important, during the community meeting, is feeding back and reflecting on what has gone on in the previous day. In that meeting, not only do the 'Top Three' feedback the content of the 'Summit' discussion but also there are standing items for the whole community, independently, to do so. As mentioned above, a written record of all emergency meetings, made by the General Secretary, is also read out prior to this communal feedback, lest important events from yesterday are forgotten or ignored. Missing more than 10 minutes of any group meeting necessitates the absenting client to provide an account to the whole community in the next day's community meeting. Thus, a client may be apprehended, challenged and supported well before needing to deploy their usual maladaptive behaviour.

Having creative and healthy outlets for pent up energies is crucial. 'Playing', as defined by Winnicott, is an activity, physical as well as mental, which is unavailable to most Henderson clients, 'because the body becomes physically involved' (Winnicott, 1958). Many are unable to 'get excited while playing, and to feel satisfied with the game, without feeling threatened by a physical orgasm of local excitement' (ibid.). Their impulsivity may be closely related to not being able to discriminate between one-off surge of excitement and the continuity of enjoyment. The TC thus provides them with many opportunities for collaborative (group) activities. This includes, importantly, physical sports activity that also affords the opportunity for playing to develop over time. Facilitating the development of a capacity to play is hard work! So there are 'Community Projects' (monthly), and a whole afternoon (also once per month) in which the community can elect to do, pretty much, as it pleases - but as a community, i.e. a large 'group'.

Ideally, some 'activity' is planned at least a bit in advance. In practice, much of what transpires is carried on with a Protestant work ethic, or else in a rebellion against it, and not with any expectation of satisfaction or self-absorption in the activity. This is in spite of there being elected clients whose job is to think about 'Sports and Social' activities on behalf of the community and to feedback these weekly into the community meeting. Frequently, little happens in the way of planning and sometimes an anticipated pleasurable event is undermined by a 'crisis', with its associated emergency meeting (see above), timed to perfection to scupper the potential for the community to 'play'. Yet, all of this defensive activity is again grist to the community's psychotherapeutic mill!

Psychodrama, Art Therapy and the 'Work Groups' are also potential opportunities to be physically active and to learn to play (Hamer, 1993). Some clients do learn to have a different experience therein and some also surprise even themselves to find they have talents hitherto undiscovered. It is sometimes unclear, however, whether some strenuous and apparently conscientious digging in the garden or felling of a tree, during a Work Group, is undertaken in the intended spirit or in the service of otherwise unexpressed anger- burying or toppling some hate figure from the past- 'a physical orgasm of local excitement'? In the daily community meeting there is a standing item relating to 'Yesterday's Groups'. This is intended to give all concerned a chance to say what happened (or did not) and, as importantly, in what spirit it was undertaken. The group setting of these treatment ingredients means that there is much opportunity for clients to witness each other working, struggling - even playing - and to identify with them. Relevant feedback may lead to a cautious experimentation with novel ways of being and doing.

Abandonment Fears: preparation for leaving

Clients such as those at Henderson, are described as having problems relating to attachment and separation, stemming from abuse and neglect in their formative years (Holmes, 1999). Therefore much attention is given to joining and leaving the TC (Norton, 1998). For example, there is a thrice-weekly group for new clients during the first three weeks of their stay. Also there is an elaborate set of group structures associated with leaving which comes into effect three months prior to the client's actual leaving date. In addition, 'Welfare Groups' are available, at least weekly, throughout the admission. Ostensibly, these groups support practical issues being discussed and resolved within a group setting but also offer an exploration of associated feelings and opportunity for the enactment of peer group support and collaboration, with professionals taking a back seat (Parker, 1989; Esterhuyzen and Winterbotham, 1998). The two main aims are: (1) to identify realistic concerns and ways to deal with these and (2) to connect these appropriate anxieties with actual events, as they are encountered. The emphasis is thus on reality-testing and avoiding a dislocation of emotional response from pressing practical issues (see 'Attacks on linking').

Support for joining and leaving is available from a multidisciplinary staff group who offer mainly a 'before and after' service in relation to the residential resource. This 'Outreach' team address concerns that became evident from an audit of ex-clients, their referrers and their GPs (Dolan and Norton 1998). All of the latter concurred that more should be done to smooth the transition of clients back into the outside world. As a result, the Outreach staff interface with residential staff working jointly in the co–facilitation of the groups specifically associated with joining and leaving (Morant et al, 1999). The so-called 'Transition Group' has already been referred to and is worthy of separate mention.

This group comprises clients due to leave in three months or less, plus those who have left (in the previous six months) after a completed stay, generally meaning having stayed beyond nine months and having left in a planned, rather than an impulsive, manner. As above, the group is facilitated by staff from both limbs of the Henderson service (residential and Outreach) to maximise continuity, thereby smoothing the transition period. The main issue is that of leaving and this involves both practical and emotional concerns and, specifically, it aims to integrate the two, maintaining a balance between them and losing sight of neither one, i.e. resisting attacks on linking. In practice, linking is difficult to achieve. Leaving is painful and regression to earlier modes of coping, on the basis of abandonment fears that re-surface, is common. However, this group, which has evolved over time, seems to be supportive and successful in bringing into consciousness just how painful the leaving process can be, how much support of whatever kind might be required, how much it might be realistically available and from whom.

Previously, in the absence of those who had actually experienced leaving, it was more difficult to help the group form a realistic view of what was required in re-negotiating with the outside world. There was thus a tendency either to deny the painful reality that the TC would be left, or to form a catastrophic – abandonment - view of the future beyond Henderson. Each of these polarised views led to under-planning and the need to act at the last minute i.e. to repeat earlier impulsive patterns. As might be expected, there is a weekly slot in the relevant community meeting for feedback from and to those preparing to leave. In this way this client sub-system is helped to have its issues recognised realistically - not minimised or exaggerated. This agenda item also serves to allow non-leaving members a chance to learn vicariously how they might be affected when their own time comes to leave.

Conclusion

A cursory look at Henderson's timetable does not convey the experience of continuity that evolves among the residents in the TC, from one 24 hours period to the next. In effect, treatment in a residential TC offers an experience of almost continuous therapy, albeit a year-long, at times structured, and often highly complex living-learning environment. Within this, there is a rich mixture of formal and informal (unstructured) ingredients. Moreover, the smaller groups, which each client joins, comprise a slightly different, though overlapping, membership. This means that the experience is one, throughout the day, of repeatedly joining and leaving groups- attaching and separating. Integral to this is the need to adapt to a changing set of roles, responsibilities and expectations with each new group and situation encountered.

For Henderson's clients, there may be something intrinsically therapeutic in encountering such a predictable but complex social situation - one that represents many of the personal and interpersonal tasks and challenges of ordinary psychological and social development. De Mare has suggested that both small and median groups are required if not only family but also societal problems are to be adequately addressed in therapy (de Mare, 1985). This is what is on offer within the residential, democratic TC. The client encounters a vast array of tasks and settings but within a knowable framework, so that the environment is predictable, at least to a degree. Through encountering this, many of the core difficulties are identified (often via their personal, interpersonal or social enactment) and space is provided for reflection on their origins and consequences, so as to maximise the possibility of change.

The groups are all 'slow open' but, as far as possible, with specific staff who are regularly assigned. There are in excess of 20 group meetings in a given week, not all shown on the timetable and not counting emergency meetings. Some emphasise 'talking' (e.g. small psychotherapy groups), others 'doing' (e.g. work groups, art therapy and psychodrama). Some are highly structured and 'chaired', such as, the community meeting. Others allow for freer expression and spontaneous interaction, notably the emergency meetings. The unstructured time allows for social involvement through carrying out the duties associated with 'jobs', as well as presenting opportunities to experiment with new interpersonal styles of relating during free time. Altogether, the clients are exposed to differing modes of experiencing themselves and others. Through these myriad encounters, they become subject to a mixture of influences- validating, corrective and socialising.

It will be clear from the above discussion that a detailed look at an individual treatment ingredient is of itself not meaningful and may be potentially misleading. Only considering it in its combination can the array of group meetings begin to make sense. In their operation, it is only with close scrutiny (by clients and the staff in collaboration), leading to their flexible alignment, that any therapeutic potential can be realised. It is an ever-present possibility that a dislocation of one group from its after-group or from another group, or the divorce of the 'social' time from the structured time of the group programme will result, rendering the 'whole' meaningless, offering no food for thought nor space for real reflection.

In the pursuit of making meaningful connections, it should be noted that: (1) an emergency meeting can interrupt any other meeting, formal or informal; and (2) it is the speed with which this meeting can be instigated, mobilising the total community resources that matters. Such prompt community action is potentially containing as well as therapeutic and, at the same time, it is minimising of risk. This capacity, to minimise risk at the same time as containing emotional and interpersonal conflict, represents the enactment of a 'holding' environment (Winnicott, 1968; Norton and Dolan, 1995). Such an environment, which also avoids being intrusive and infantilising, facilitates a psychosocial maturation of the client, bringing with it a potential for symbolic living and not simple survival.

Hospitals reflect one of society's main attempts to care for and heal itself. Many of these specialised institutions have developed out of the work of pioneering individuals, whose charismatic leadership generated and supported a group of like-minded souls (Manning, 1989). This is so for the modern era of therapeutic milieus within mental health services. Maxwell Jones' observation, that the clients could be more influential in inducing a real change in attitudes and behaviour than could professionals, including himself, set the scene for one strand of the development of the democratic TC (Jones, 1946). This type of institution, constructed from an active and ongoing participation of clients in collaboration with professionals, became inevitably client-centred to an unprecedented degree.

Jones' Unit, originally sited in a large mental hospital and now named Henderson Hospital, became relatively autonomous with the demise of the parent organisation and gradually focused on the treatment of Personality Disorder clients, using only group methods (Whiteley, 1980). By the late 1960s much of its current general structure, in terms of its formal programme of group meetings, was in place. Fashioned by a high level of client input it provides a clinical environment exquisitely tailored to the specific needs of people with personality disorder. Core aspects of their psychosocial pathology can therefore be evoked and addressed. New coping strategies can be tried and the results of such experimentation fed back into the formal group structure for further exploration and refinement. To achieve the ambitious aim of ego development, in the sense described above (from actors/non-feelers to thinkers/feelers), there has developed a wide range of group types. Together, they offer the potential ingredients for change. However, much can still go wrong in the blending of the group ingredients, especially in the heat of the large crucible of the community and emergency meetings!

For most of the time, staff need to delegate to their clients much of their traditional power and status, in favour of a collaborative and democratic approach. This is not easy to do. It requires of them more than a tokenistic acceptance that, however disordered the clients, they are people who have strengths and who, under the peculiar arrangement and operation of the TC's group system, can acquire psychosocial skills and a lessening of reliance on self-destructive or antisocial defences. To this end, staff also require an elaborate group structure in order to obtain adequate support and supervision and to maintain interpersonal sensitivity. This is so that they can improve their skills in identifying when an authentic 'culture of enquiry' (into the personal, interpersonal and social systems of the TC) has been lost, either transiently or longer term, and how this might be restored.

One year in the stressful and stimulating, 'living-learning' environment of the TC can be life-changing and research shows encouraging findings (Whiteley, 1970; Copas et al 1984; Dolan et al, 1992; Dolan et al 1996; Dolan et al, 1997; Norton and Warren, in press), although Henderson has not been subjected to the test of a randomised controlled trial. The TC is as supportive as it is challenging for those who successfully engage. However, its therapeutic effect cannot be taken for granted. Ultimately, the therapeutic agent is the 'community' itself. Ideally, this functions with sufficient cohesion and flexibility as to be experienced as a containing and transforming 'other' that is never off duty. On a good day, it remembers your name and notices when you're not there!

Acknowlegements

Oded Manor, who requested this contribution to *Groupwork*, assisted me in providing many helpful amendments to the text, which have improved the end product and made it much more intelligible and readable – you might imagine what it was like before! For this I thank him.

References

American Psychiatric Association (1994) *Diagnostic and Statistical Manual of Mental Disorder, IV.* Washington, DC: American Psychiatric Association Press

Bion, W.R. (1961) *Experiences in Groups.* London: Heinemann

Bion, W.R. (1963) *Elements of Psychoanalysis.* London: Heinemann

Clarke, D. (1965) The therapeutic community: concept, practice and future. *British Journal of Psychiatry*, 111, 947-954

Copas, J.B., O'Brien, M., Roberts, and J.C., Whiteley, J.S. (1984) Treatment outcome in personality disorder: The effect of social, psychological and behavioural variables. *Personality and Individual Differences*, 5, 565-573

De Mare, P. (1985) Large group perspectives. *Group Analysis*, 17/2, 79-92

Dolan, B., Morton, A., and Wilson, J. (1990) Selection of admissions to a therapeutic community using a group setting: Association with degree and type of psychological distress. *International Journal of Social Psychiatry*, 36, 4, 265-271

Dolan, B., Evans, C., and Wilson, J. (1992) Therapeutic community treatment for personality disordered adults: Changes in neurotic symptomatology on follow-up. *International Journal of Social Psychiatry*, 38, 4, 243-250

Dolan, B., Warren, F., Menzies, D., and Norton, K. (1996) Cost-offset following specialist treatment of severe personality disorders. *Psychiatric Bulletin*, 20, 7

Dolan, B., Warren, F., and Norton, K. (1997) Change in borderline symptoms one year after therapeutic community treatment for severe personality disorder. *British Journal of Psychiatry*, 171, 274-279

Dolan, B. and Norton, K. (1998) Audit and survival: Specialist in-patient psychotherapy in the NHS. in M. Patrick and R. Davenhill (Eds.) *Reconstructing Audit: The case of psychotherapy services in the NHS*. London: Routledge,

Erikson, E. H. (1956) The problem of ego identity. *Journal of the American Psychoanalytical Association*. 4, 56-121

Esterhuyzen, A. and Winterbotham M. (1998) Surfing the Interface: How to Make a Welfare Group a Microcosm of Therapeutic Community Functioning. *Therapeutic Communities*, 19, 4, 295-305

Gabbard, G.O. (1988) A contemporary perspective on psychoanalytically informed hospital treatment. *Hospital Community Psychiatry*, 39, 1291-5

Gray, W., Duhl, F.J., and Rizzo, N.D. (Eds.) (1969) *General Systems Theory and Psychiatry*. Boston: Little Brown

Gunderson, J.G. (1978) Defining the therapeutic processes in psychiatric milieus. *Psychiatry*, 41, 327-335

Hamer, N. (1993) Some connections between art therapy and psychodrama in a therapeutic community. *Inscape: Journal of the British Association of Art Therapists*. Winter, 23-26

Hinshelwood, R. D. (1979) The community as analyst. in R.D. Hinshelwood and N. Manning (Eds.) *Therapeutic Communities*. pp.103-112. London: Routledge and Keagan Paul

Holmes, J. (1999) Psychotherapeutic approaches to the management of severe personality disorder in general psychiatric settings. *Rila Publications, CPD Bulletin Psychiatry*, 1, 2, 29-68

Jones, M. (1946) Rehabilitation of forces neurosis patients to civilian life. *British Medical Journal*, 6, 533-535

Jones, M. (1952) *Social Psychiatry: A study of therapeutic communities.* London: Tavistock Pub

Kernberg, O. (1966) Structural derivatives of object relationships. *International Journal of Psychoanalysis*, 47, 236-253

Kernberg, O (1984) *Severe Personality Disorders.* New Haven: Yale University press:

Main, T. (1946) The hospital as a therapeutic institution. *Bulletin of the Menninger Clinic*, 10, 66-68

Main, T. (1983) The concept of the therapeutic community: Variations and vicissitudes. in M. Pine (Ed.) *The Evolution of Group Analysis*. London: Routledge & Kegan Paul

Manning, N. (1989) *The Therapeutic Community Movement: Charisma and routinization.* London: Routledge,

Mahoney, M. (1979) My stay and change at the Henderson therapeutic community. in R. Hinshelwood and N. Manning (Eds) *Therapeutic Communities: Reflections and Progress.* pp 76-87, London: Routledge,

Masterson, J. (1972) *Treatment of the Borderline Adolescent: A developmental approach.* New York: Wiley

Miller, L.J. (1989) Inpatient management of borderline personality disorder: a review and update. *Journal of Personality Disorders*, 3, 122-134

Morant, N., Dolan, B., Fainman, D., and Hilton, M. (1999) An innovative outreach service for people with severe personality disorders: Patient characteristics and clinical activities. *Journal of Forensic Psychiatry*, 10, 1, 84-97

Norton, K. (1992) Personality disordered individuals: the Henderson Hospital model of treatment. *Criminal behaviour and Mental Health*, 2, 180-191

Norton, K., and Dolan, B. (1995) A culture of enquiry, its preservation or loss. *Therapeutic Communities*, 1, 1, 3-26

Norton, K., and Dolan, B. (1995) Acting out and the institutional response. *Journal of Forensic Psychiatry*, 6, 2, 317-332

Norton, K. (1996) The personality disordered forensic patient and the therapeutic community. in M. Cox and C. Cordess (Eds.) *Forensic*

Psychotherapy. London: Jessica Kingsley

Norton, K. and Dolan, B. (1996) Personality disorders and their effect upon parenting. in M. Gopfert, J. Webster, and M. Seeman (Eds.) *Mentally Disordered Parents*, (pp.219-232) Cambridge: Cambridge University Press

Norton, K. and Hinshelwood, R. (1996) Severe personality disorder: Treatment issues and selection for inpatient psychotherapy. *British Journal of Psychiatry*, 168, 6, 725-733

Norton, K. (1997a) Inpatient psychotherapy: integrating the other 23 hours. (Comment) *Current Medical Literature*, 8, 2, 31-37

Norton, K. (1997b) In the prison of severe personality disorder. *The Journal of Forensic Psychiatry*, 8, 2, 285-298

Norton, K. (1998) Joining and leaving: Processing separation, loss and re-attachment. In R. Haigh, and P. Campling (Eds.) *Therapeutic Communities: Past, present and future*. London: Jessica Kingsley

Norton, K., and Haigh, R. (2001) The Therapeutic Community: Theoretical, practical and therapeutic integration. in A. Bateman, and J. Holmes, (Eds.) *Theory, Models and Practice*. (pp.159-174) Oxford: Oxford University Press

Norton, K., and Warren, F. (in press) Assessment and outcome in therapeutic communities: Challenges and achievements. in J. Lees, N. Manning, D. Menzies, and N. Morant, (Eds) *Researching Therapeutic Communities*. London: Jessica Kingsley

Parker, M. (1989) Managing Separation: The Henderson hospital leavers group. *International Journal of Therapeutic Communities*. 8, 1, 21-31

Rapoport, R. (1960) *Community as Doctor*. London: Tavistock

Roberts, J.P. (1980) Destructive processes in a therapeutic community. *International Journal of Therapeutic Communities*, 1, 3, 159-170

Rothman, D.J. (1980) *Conscience and Convenience*. Glenview, IL: Scott and Foresman Von Bertalannfy (1967) General systems theory and psychiatry. in S Arieti (Ed.) *The Foundations of Psychiatry: American handbook of psychiatry*. Volume 1. New York: Basic Books

Whiteley, J.S. (1970) The response of psychopaths to a therapeutic community. *British Journal of Psychiatry*, 116, 517-529

Whiteley, J.S. (1980) The Henderson hospital: A community study. *International Journal of Therapeutic Communities*, 1, 1, 38-57

Whiteley, J.S. (1986) Sociotherapy and psychotherapy in the treatment of personality disorder. *Journal of the Royal Society of Medicine*, 79, 721-5

Whiteley, J.S., and Collis, M. (1987) Therapeutic factors applied to group psychotherapy in a therapeutic community. *International Journal of Therapeutic Communities*, 8, 21-31

Winnicott, D.W. (1958) The capacity to be alone. in D.W. Winnicott *The Maturational Processes and the Facilitating Environment.* London: The Hogarth Press

Winnicott, D.W. (1965) *The Maturational Processes and the Facilitating Environment.* London: Hogarth

Winnicott, D.W. (1968) The use of an object and relating through identifications. in *Playing and Reality*, pp.86-94. London: Tavistock, 1971

This chapter was first published in 2003 in *Groupwork* Vol. 13(3), pp.65-100

At the time of writing, Dr Kingsley Norton was Director, Henderson Hospital and Reader in Psychotherapy, St George's Hospital Medical School

Groupwork fit for purpose? An inclusive framework for mental health

Oded Manor[1]

How can we make groupwork relevant to current community mental health? This paper is a call for action research into the different contributions of groupwork to this field. It is suggested that we can identify specific goals for each group member by asking members which quality of life goals they want to pursue. We can then analyse the learning experiences that may promote each of these goals.

Three major learning experiences seem to match three major approaches to groupwork practice. Furthermore, the dynamics emphasised by each of these three approaches appears to be similar to the dynamics of three well known phases of group development. Therefore, it may be possible to offer a very diverse range of groupwork methods in advancing very different quality of life goals.

Such diversity does not necessarily lead to fragmentation of groupwork as a whole. Anchoring groupwork in the inclusive stance may enable us to clarify similarities and differences among the various approaches. Such an inclusive venture may help make groupwork more fit for purpose.

Key words: *quality of life goals; learning experience; group development*

Introduction

Mental health practice in Britain has undergone considerable changes in recent years. Practitioners have been directed to concentrate mainly on helping clients with severe and enduring mental health problems, to do so within the Care Programme Approach and organise this work through community mental health teams (Bleach and Ryan, 1995; Brooker and Repper, 1998; DoH, 1995; DoH, 1999; 1998; Forster, 1997; Onyett, 2003).

In this context is groupwork fit for purpose? How can groupwork be applied in this new era?

Indeed, the range of group methods is now vast. In this paper I shall offer a definition of *groupwork* as distinct from other forms of working with groups. These include group psychotherapy (MacKenzie, 1997), practice with networks (Lin and Peck, 1999) or work in organisations (Hartley, 1997; Morgan 1997; Onyett et al., 1996; Pearson and Spencer, 1995).

Essentially, this paper is a call for action research into the different contributions that groupwork can make to the quality of life of mental health clients.

It will be suggested that:

- Quality of life goals may not be of one mould, and so - different goals may be pursued through different learning experiences.
- If clients need different learning experiences in pursuing different goals then we shall have to draw on different groupwork methods when working on each goal. But this diversity does not have to lead to open-ended eclecticism.
- It may be possible to cluster groupwork methods into three major types. These three clusters seem to be similar to the dynamics of three major stages of group development.
- If the similarity between groupwork methods and groupwork phases is valid, then an overall framework can be found to connect and separate methods according to the quality of life goals of its members.

Such an analysis can be the first stage of ensuring that groupwork is fit for current purposes. As will be shown, no groupwork method will be rejected: psychosocial approaches will have their place, social groupwork will be recognised and groups for personal growth will be respected too. Rather, the contribution of each to promoting different quality of life goals will be identified, and the connections among them clarified. Such connections will ensure that the proposed framework is inclusive.

Before explaining this proposal, a few words about the context of practice seem to be needed.

Context and aims

Many have written about groupwork practice in great detail. Distinct models have been suggested: for example, cognitive-behavioural therapy for specific psychiatric symptoms (Scott and Stradling, 1998), skill training (Trower et al., 1978), the use of activities while focusing on clients' role and occupation (Finlay, 1997; Finlay, 2000) and certainly mutual aid (Doel and Sawdon, 2000, p.67). The point is that these methods, and others, have to be applied within the Care Programme Approach by community mental health teams that are inter-professional.

Secker et al. (2000) and particularly Freeman et al. (2000) have already identified the assortment of interests and philosophies that seem to whirl around in community mental health teams. These teams organise the service according to the principles of the Care Programme Approach (Bleach and Ryan, 1995; Forster, 1997). Therefore, the groupwork methods must be fit for the purposes pursued by such teams.

Experience suggests that many obstacles stand in the way of rigorously applying groupwork. The accounts I have received as a journal editor, a consultant, and an examiner suggest that practitioners do not always appreciate the particular advantages of groupwork, and many lack specific training in applying this method. In our study of mental health practitioners in south London, (Papps et al., 2003) it appeared that those who had worked with groups during the previous twelve months did so more because they were convinced of the merit of groupwork than due to the support they had been offered. Indeed, those who had not offered groupwork cited difficulties in fitting groupwork into their existing caseload as the prime reason.

These problems are likely to impede the use of groupwork in mental health elsewhere. However, in this paper I shall not discuss all these stumbling blocks. Instead, I shall concentrate on one other problem: the disparate nature of practice.

The Care Programme Approach rightly requires us to identify specific goals in our work with clients, and monitor the extent that these goals are achieved. However, to pursue such goals in practice we need also to articulate the *means* of achieving them. Yet, at present, it is not really easy to map out the various contributions of groupwork in this respect.

This is a rich source of contributions, but these are not coherently mapped out yet.

How can we clarify the goals of groupwork more specifically and choose the methods of pursuing each goal more purposefully?

A solution is needed that addresses three major aims:

- Find indicators that can be used by all to *systematically evaluate* the extent that each group member is progressing towards achieving a specific goal.
- Identify the learning experiences that may help members pursue each of these goals.
- Match these learning experiences to known groupwork methods.
- Ground all these groupwork methods in one conceptual framework to ensure that differences and similarities among them can be mapped out.

I shall suggest how we may advance the last three aims step-by-step. As I do this, I shall comment on the first aim: building into the framework mechanisms that enable the systematic evaluation of practice.

The first step can be to identify clients' diverse needs more specifically. It seems to me that the concept of 'quality of life' can be rather helpful in this.

Quality of life

Clients' quality of life can be the major target of groupwork interventions. The term is as evocative as it is loose (Priebe et al., 1999). Indeed, quality of life is hard to conceptualise – one person's judgement may be very different from that of another when identifying 'the good life' (Oliver et al., 1996, pp.15-47). After reviewing the various possibilities, these authors settled for a pragmatic selection of aspects. Those aspects were medical, psychological and social. All were concerned with the client's well being, and were identified by mental health clients as well as professionals as relevant, while also being amenable to systematic examination. Oliver et al. (1996, p.17) add that: 'Quality of life measurements are sufficiently wide to encompass many perspectives, proving acceptable to a range of different practitioners and thus encouraging teamwork'.

This particular definition is certainly not ideal, but it has been shown to be helpful in a very wide range of studies (Priebe et al., 1999). Therefore, at this stage, the framework suggested by Oliver et al. (1996) will be adopted as an example.

The framework has been operationalised through the Lancashire Quality of Life Profile (Oliver et al., 1996, pp.251-264). In practice, practitioners can ask each client to complete the questionnaire before joining the group, at the end of the group and at a follow-up date. Therefore, the data gathered can provide a systematic profile of each client's progress. These are the headings of the Lancashire Quality of Life Profile:

- *Work/education:* Whether client is employed and the client's satisfaction in this regard.
- *Leisure/participation:* Client's leisure activities and satisfaction derived from these.
- *Religion:* Client's religious affiliation, frequency of attending religious activities and satisfaction derived.
- *Finances:* Client's income and satisfaction with this situation.
- *Living situation:* Client's living conditions and satisfaction with these.
- *Legal and safety:* Client's involvement in crime: As a victim or a perpetrator, and client's satisfaction with the situation.
- *Family relations:* Marital and familial status, participation in family activities and satisfaction with these.
- *Social relations:* The nature of friendship in which client is involved and client's satisfaction with these relations.
- *Health:* Client's involvement with medical professionals and satisfaction related to such involvement.
- *Self-concept:* Client's feeling of self-worth.
- *General well-being:* Client's overall feeling about his/her life and the extent that client's hopes have been fulfilled.

In our study (Papps et al., 2003) of mental health practitioners in South London, practitioners acknowledged the importance of all these goals, but not all of them equally. For example, promoting clients' positive self-concept was highest on their agenda, while helping clients with legal matters was the lowest.

The greatest advantage of identifying these goals is that these can be monitored systematically.

The question is what may help clients achieve each of these goals? By mapping out the learning experiences that seem relevant to pursuing different quality of life goals some directions may be suggested.

Learning experiences as a guide

Indeed, the various ways people learn has been studied for a long time. One of the relevant and most established approaches is Kolb's (1984) model of experiential learning. The model of experiential learning (Kolb, 1984, p.30) suggests that four aspects are involved:

- 'Reflective observation': when people 'reflect on and observe their experiences from many perspectives'. Here these experiences can be simply called 'reflecting'.
- 'Abstract conceptualization': when learners 'create concepts that integrate their observations into logically sound theories'. For the present purpose the term 'conceptualising' seems adequate.
- 'Active experimentation': when people 'use these theories to make decisions and solve problems'. The term 'experimenting' seems to capture this aspect in the present context.
- 'Concrete experience': when people 'involve themselves fully, openly, and without bias in new experiences'. In the present context this will amount to 'applying' what they learn in their daily lives.

The exact manifestation of each of these aspects will vary according to the context of learning (Manor, 1988; 1990), and the order in which learners are engaged in each is not always the same

(Tsang, 1990). However, one advantage of Kolb's method is that it can be used to identify learning styles systematically.

The main question now is which combination of learning experiences may serve best in eliciting and building-up different clients' quality of life abilities. The task is to identify the various learning experiences that are relevant to pursuing different quality of life goals.

Quality of life goals and associated learning experiences

To increase specificity it is necessary to identify learning experiences that may help clients pursue different quality of life goals. Indeed, logically speaking, quality of life goals do not appear to be of one mould. Here are some examples:

Pursing the goals of 'work and education' may well involve learning how to prepare a job application and presenting oneself during job interviews. The type of learning involved is usually cognitive-behavioural: *discrete* terms are acquired and specific behaviours are identified and rehearsed. The learning experiences involved would appear linear:

- understanding the sequence of interactions that can be expected during the interview is a matter of *conceptualising*,
- clarifying one's feelings about the job and applying for it involves *reflecting*,
- rehearsing actual behaviours that may help during the interview is a form of *experimenting*, and
- actually completing the real tasks of attending the interview entails *applying* all the learning to a real life situation..

Other quality of life goals may be similar; for example, 'finance': claiming benefits, or 'health': coping with the effects of medication. The main point here is that the learning experiences involved appear *linear*. Like climbing up a ladder: a sequence of distinct experiences *can be planned step-by-step, and clients can be directed towards each – one at a time.* The sequence would begin with

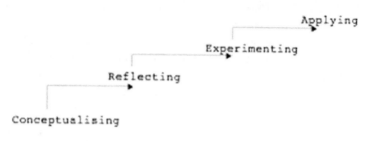

Figure 1: Linear learning: Climbing up a ladder

conceptualising, move on to reflecting, give space to experimenting and end in applying learning to daily life. This linear mode of learning is depicted in Figure 1 overleaf.

More complex are 'social relations' with their focus on interpersonal experiences. Making friends and sustaining friendship are likely to involve clients in relating to different people differently. Gender roles, age, race and culture, as well as interests may have to be taken into account. Learning to form and sustain friendships is not likely to be a matter of adopting a fixed routine. Rather, a form of interpersonal agility may be called for where the person is flexible enough to reach different people in different ways and sustain that contact with each for shorter or longer periods. I would suggest that learning experiences needed to help clients develop such agility are likely to be less structured than the cognitive-behavioural ones.

- For quite a while, clients are likely to need to *experiment* with different approaches. For example, do they say 'hello' to someone sitting next to them in the pub or wait to be approached? Do they form eye contact or turn their head down? Various possibilities exist and no fixed routine can be recommended for all occasions.
- Next will come the reactions of unknown people: if someone smiles, what does the client feel: embarrassed, encouraged, threatened? Clients will need to reflect upon their own reactions if they are to develop the agility that will enable them to sustain and develop such unexpected experiences into relationships.

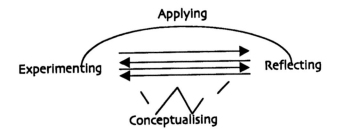

Figure 2: Interactive learning: Learning to dance

- Occasionally learning may involve also *conceptualising* these possibilities; for example – if a person does not respond does it always mean that you are rejected? What else can explain such a reaction? Group members can help one another find different explanations.
- While they do so, clients may *concurrently* apply what they learn; in the group itself and as time goes by – to more and more situations outside.

When it comes to forming and sustaining friendships, it is hard to see a linear sequence of learning experiences charted in advance and directed towards specific goals. Rather, such a goal is probably pursued by learning to improvise through continuous interaction with peers: in the group as well as outside it - in real life.

Other quality of life goals may fall under this type too; for example, 'living situation': coping with other residents in the hostel, or 'leisure': going to swim or visiting an art gallery.

All these goals appear to be mainly composite interpersonal goals where people negotiate the implications of their involvement with *peers*. Metaphorically, these experiences seem to resemble learning to dance: some steps may be prescribed and others improvised, there are known routines that you can memorise, but the action itself has to be improvised every time afresh. Through this type of interpersonal dance, group members learn to give and receive, to lead and to follow, to help and to be helped.

The learning experiences seem to call for an *interactive* stance, where experimentation and reflection take precedence, occasional conceptualising helps and application to daily life is *concurrent* – throughout the experience, as in Figure 2.

A third type of goals may be even more intricate. For example, what is involved in promoting a client's positive self-concept? Of course, this depends on each person's experience of self. For some, the self may be merely an abstract 'concept'; 'a woman', or 'a man', or 'a wage earner' or 'a lover'. For others, the 'self' may be far more complex. What about the experience of wanting to belong while yearning to be free of conventions? Can this be a 'concept' that is learnt through direct reasoning? What about the experience of succeeding in a job while rejecting the 'rat race'? Can this duality be directly taught and linearily learnt? These two examples are still relatively simple. When it comes to intimacy and sexuality, the layers of the self may be many – some more directly accessible and others hidden from awareness and shrouded in images and symbols. Struggling with these layers each person has to embark on a journey of a gradually evolving discovery.

This is why pursuing the goals related to 'positive self-concept' may be complex and, in addition, also a more comprehensive experience compared to the previous two. At times, an individual's experience of self may be a cluster of feelings, symbols and behaviour intricately associated with one another. Furthermore, some of these experiences may conflict with one another and may not be readily accessible to awareness (Manor, 1992). Connecting conscious and unconscious feelings, thoughts and behaviours is a *holistic* endeavour. Clinical practice suggests that it is such an all-embracing journey that leads to change and growth of a central image underpinning the sense of self.

To embark on such a journey clients may need the freedom to express themselves spontaneously – to say whatever they feel, and say this in their own ways. These people need to expand their awareness of themselves and, at the same time, deepen their empathy with others. Through such shuttling - to and fro, between themselves and others, a sense of self seems to grow. Therefore, the learning process may well be different from the linear and interactive experiences identified so far.

While holistic learning is facilitated:

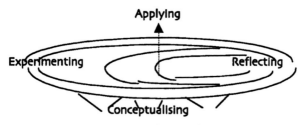

Figure 3: Experiential learning: Expanding ripples

- *Reflection* would seem to be the major learning style.
- *Experimenting* with new behaviour is likely to be encouraged as a vehicle through which further reflection can arise.
- *Conceptualising* is usually viewed only as an occasional aid, and
- *Applying* the learning to daily life is usually left to evolve according to the client's inner sense of each occasion.

Depending on the client's life styles, pursuing other quality of life goals may also require such an intricate yet contained culture; for example in exploring 'religion': client's religious experiences and involvement in organised religion, or 'family relations': particularly, participation in family activities (Sunday lunch? Family reunion?).

The learning experiences that appear relevant to pursuing such holistic goals may not be linear and may not stress interaction as much as expanding cycles of awareness. Metaphorically speaking, clients are likely to be involved in cycles of ripples of expanding awareness. In practice, the term 'experiential' is often used to refer to such cycles, and these are charted in Figure 3.

The main point is that pursuing different quality of life goals may require different learning experiences. Some experiences may be linear, others may emphasise interaction and a third may be experiential. These differences are summarised in Figure 4. Can we see these different learning experiences in the practice of groupwork?

Quality of Life Goals	Learning Experiences
Discrete e.g. work and education	Linear
Composite e.g. social relations	Interactive
Holistic e.g. self concept	Experiential

Figure 4: Nature of quality of life goals and their associated learning experiences

Groupwork and learning experiences

Elsewhere (Manor, 2000c), the wide range of groupwork applications to mental health have been mapped out. These applications are practised in different settings: psychiatric hospitals and day centres, as well as in the open community. Actual practice varies too: some emphasise structured interventions and others stress spontaneous processes. Unfortunately, the details of matching groupwork methods to quality of life goals have not been examined systematically yet. To do so, groupwork itself has to be defined first.

Many mental health practitioners are familiar with the methods of group psychotherapy (for an overall review, see MacKenzie, 1997). The aims of group psychotherapy are usually all-encompassing. Undoing the impact of past disabling relationships is as important as enhancing present coping strategies within these methods. Yalom (1995, pp.69-105) identified thirteen 'curative factors' of group psychotherapy. In groupwork, not all of these are emphasised. There is a natural overlap between group psychotherapy and groupwork, but also some distinct differences. Seven of the 'curative factors' identified by Yalom seem particularly relevant to groupwork. These are: altruism, group cohesion, universality, interpersonal learning, guidance, identification and instillation of hope.

In addition, groupwork offers each member the potential of

meeting people who can help that person outside the session – in everyday life. Effective groupwork sows the seeds of informal networks of *mutual aid* among its members (Gitterman and Shulman, 1994; Manor, 2000b), and these networks are known to ease mental health difficulties considerably (Hardcastle et al., 1997; Hatzimitriadou, 2002).

Indeed, groupwork has been defined in many different ways. For the purpose of the present discussion groupwork will be seen as:

- the work done by at least one professional,
- with at least three group members (clients or carers),
- who meet face-to-face regularly,
- become more aware of their relationships,
- while focusing on their roles in the group as well as outside it, and
- taking active part in changing these roles to enhance members' quality of life .

This definition is derived from a broader one, which is discussed elsewhere (Manor, 2000a, pp.33-38). The emphasis here is on exploring and altering interpersonal roles and eliciting members' strengths so as to enhance their quality of life. This emphasis means that groupwork will tend to focus on overcoming clients' 'negative symptoms': the difficulties they have in enhancing their quality of life (Barlow and Durand, 1995).

How may these benefits be promoted?

The question is whether the three major learning experiences: linear, interactive and experiential, can be identified within various forms of groupwork practice.

Indeed, clients' experiences may change over the lifetime of each group, and practitioners may combine various approaches for each group. Still, emphasising a particular aspect indicates a choice that marks each groupwork approach as distinct from the others.

Here are three of the major alternatives:

Directive methods

In some groupwork approaches the practitioner determines the subjects discussed, offers explanations relevant to the subject and directs the members to the contents of the exchanges among them throughout the lifetime of the group. By doing so, the practitioner constructs distinct learning experiences. Within these approaches the practitioner is in a *central* position and can be said to be in the role of *director*. Such a directive stance characterises mainly psycho-educational groups (Brown, 1998) and cognitive-behavioural group counselling (Scott and Stradling, 1998). Coming from occupational therapy, Kaplan (1988, p.41) writes:

> The group is structured around a sequence of events. When planning, first think through each segment and analyse the activities for each part individually. Then, before plunging ahead, review the sequence as a cohesive whole.

The advantages of directive methods are that these allow members to focus on bits and pieces of isolated behaviours and/or isolated and specific cognitive constructs. Members can then alter these in a planned fashion: conceptualising the change required, reflecting upon the impact of change, experimenting with new possibilities and then – applying these to daily life.

These directive and *structured* approaches seem to emphasise the linear learning described before. Therefore, it stands to reason that directive methods may be particularly relevant to pursuing discrete quality of life goals such as 'work and education'. This may be so because these goals can be broken down to small steps, such as completing job applications or applying for further education, admission interviews to a college or job interviews. Climbing these various ladders can be done step-by-step; that is, linearily. Other goals are probably similar. Examples may include: 'finance'; as while claiming benefits, 'health'; when asking the GP about side effects of medication, and 'legal and safety'; as in understanding tenancy rights.

Mediating methods

The practitioner can invite group members to choose the contents of the sessions themselves instead of directing their discussion. When the practitioner adopts such a position far more interaction is likely to arise among the members of the group. Practice experience suggests that members then have to learn how to allocate speaking time for everybody, and how to deal with differences among themselves. When such degree of choice is left in members' hands power relations among them are likely to come to the surface. The practitioner who invites such a degree of choice opts for an *intermediate* rather than a central position in the group and enters the role of *mediator.*

Indeed, social group work has a long tradition of fostering mediating methods; mainly through mutual aid groups. Shulman (1999, p.315) explains that:

> In many ways the group practitioner serves as a guide for the group faced with the complex task of developing an effective mutual aid system.

Structured activities chosen by members are also used in the Club House approach (Oliver et al., pp.209-222), as well as some forms of self-help groups (Wilson, 1995). From this perspective, the 'self-directed' model developed by Mullender and Ward (1991) also belongs here. This model simply extends the momentum of mutual aid to enable the group as a whole to 'take action for empowerment'. The focus of empowerment in these groups is in relation to larger; often statutory, bodies. Indeed, the thrust of 'users' involvement' finds its clearest expression in these groups.

While the methods emphasise group members' involvement at different levels, all tend to foster a culture in which free interaction is negotiated among peers.

Indeed, such free interaction is not enabled for its own sake. As already suggested, free interaction may be needed in pursuing *composite* quality of life goal such as 'social relations'. Goals related to 'living situations' and to 'leisure' may be of a similar nature.

Pursuing such goals, group members have to spend considerable time *experimenting* with and *reflecting* upon alternative ways of relating to people. *Conceptualising* is only occasionally ventured. Yet, *applying* learning to everyday life is concurrent. In short, the 'interactive' learning experiences mentioned before seem most relevant.

Facilitative methods

A practitioner may not choose to be directive nor to mediate. Instead, she can keep changing her responses according to the ever-changing experiences each member experiences in the here-and-now of the group. At times, such a practitioner may focus on showing that she is listening and on communicating empathy. At others, the practitioner may actively focus members' emotional expressions and help to clarify their meaning. Throughout, the facilitative practitioner keeps following the flow of spontaneous processes. This practitioner seems to opt for a *variable* position and to adopt the role of *facilitator*.

Such a style of working stems mainly from the seminal work of Rogers (1970) and contemporary examples can be seen in group counselling texts such as those by Berg et al. (1998) and Trotzer (1999). As one practitioner writes:

> I would like to gently touch each member's emotional world .... I would like the total response of my person to convey to the group member the depth of my yearning to know and understand, to the extent to which I am fully capable, his or her experiential inner world of feelings and thoughts as known, experienced, felt, expressed and lived out at the moment. (Berg et al., 1998, pp.50)

At a far less intensely personal level, 'activity-based' centres (Oliver et al., 1996, pp.179-186) and drop-in clubs can be said to enable a certain level of such containment too. Truly facilitative approaches may be particularly relevant to pursuing more *holistic* quality of life goals such as those related to members' self-concept. Issues concerned with 'religion' as well as some of the more intimate aspects 'family relations' may be addressed in this manner too.

Indeed, full reading of practice accounts suggests that the learning experiences within facilitative methods emphasise *reflecting. Experimenting* with new expressions is seen as an aide to further reflection. *Conceptualising* is only an occasional concern and *application* to daily life is expected to grow as and when each member is ready for it. In this sense, facilitative methods seem to engender the learning experiences identified here as '*experiential*'.

As can be seen, the three clusters are quite different from one another, and each may serve a different purpose. Figure 5 summarises the suggestions put forward so far.

Figure 5: Quality of life goals, learning experiences and groupwork methods

Quality of Life Goals	Learning Experiences	Groupwork method
discrete	linear	directive
composite	interactive	mediating
holistic	experiential	facilitative

Looking at Figure 5 may well lead to a crucial question: is this diversity destroying coherence? Is this leading to breaking up of groupwork into isolated chunks of technical knowledge? Will the practice of groupwork appear to others too disjointed?

If this happens care managers may not be able to know how to incorporate groupwork into a coherent care programme, nor how to evaluate the methods that may best help each client achieve their goal. Indeed, judging by the impressions received from the field this may actually be the state of groupwork to date. This is one possible explanation for the apparent unplanned uses of groupwork in current mental health practice.

I would suggest that diversity does not necessarily lead to chaos and fragmentation. One way of overcoming fragmentation may emerge when we look at the picture as a whole. Seen as a whole, the three methods appear to reflect stages of group development.

Groupwork methods as stages of group development

The practitioner may direct, or mediate or facilitate group relationships. In each role the practitioner is likely to engender different learning experiences. In groupwork these experiences are summarised by the term 'group dynamics'.

Of course, the dynamics that emerge in the group over time have been observed and analysed for many decades (Lacoursiere, 1980). Many observers have noticed that, at times, certain processes lead to group dynamics coalescing around a certain level; for example: social, interpersonal or personal, and around a certain theme; for example, trust, or power or intimacy. When such a convergence occurs it is described as a *stage* of group development.

Groups set up to pursue different goals tend to develop through different stages. Indeed, the inclusive blueprint of group stages (Manor, 2000a) was constructed to deal with this fact. The blueprint is an overall framework that accounts for all the potential stages that may emerge. At the same time, this blueprint enables each practitioner to choose only the stages that reflect the needs of group members with which they work. Yet, fragmentation is not encouraged, as all practitioners are expected to work within a single unifying framework: resorting to the same terms when making their own individual choices.

The inclusive framework of group stages may be helpful here. This may be so because *when the phases of the inclusive blueprint are examined, each appears to correspond to one of the clusters of groupwork approaches mentioned above.* Here are major possibilities:

Directive methods and the engagement phase

As discussed before, the dynamics of *directive methods* involve the practitioner in a central position, from which she directs linear learning.

Indeed, within the inclusive framework (for a definition and an example, see Manor, 2000a, pp.104-117) adopting such a central position is typical of the practitioner's stance during the first stage, called the 'Engagement phase'. During the Engagement phase the practitioner remains in a central position. The practitioner focuses on directing the group - generating trust and engaging members in topics that are relevant to all members. Consequently, members' learning experiences are likely to be linear: one follows the other in the order deemed appropriate by the practitioner.

Therefore, the proposed research may examine the possibility that directive methods extend the dynamics of the Engagement phase and turn these into the major mode of learning until the group ends at the Termination phase.

Mediating methods and the empowerment phase

As already noted, the dynamics of *mediating methods* involve the practitioner in an intermediate position, from which she mediates interaction.

This mediating role of the practitioner resembles the involvement of practitioners in the second phase of the inclusive blueprint, called 'the Empowerment phase' (for a definition and an example, see Manor, 2000a, pp.132-143). During the Empowerment phase group members choose the contents to be discussed or the activity to be pursued. They are then busy learning how to share power with others: inside as well as outside the group. Learning occurs mainly through interaction among the members, until the termination phase - when the group ends.

As can be expected, the mediating method begins with relationships that resemble the Engagement phase of the inclusive blueprint. However, the mediating practitioner is expected to shift to an intermediate position as soon as the group is ready for this. This shift is needed because the 'work' of the group is expected to occur mainly through interaction among the members themselves. Therefore, when further examined, mediating methods may appear to extend the Empowerment phase so that it becomes the major dynamics for most of the group's life.

Facilitative methods and the mutuality phase

It was also suggested that within facilitative methods the practitioner shifts to a variable position as soon as it is viable, from which she enables experiential learning.

This is also true for the Mutuality phase (for a definition and an example, see Manor, 2000a, pp.159-179). During such a period facilitative practitioners tend to change their relationship with members as and when required. These practitioners adopt a variable position so they can be flexible enough to respond to spontaneous verbal and bodily expressions in the group. Sometimes they work behind the scene and at others they actively intervene to mobilise more genuine expressions of feelings, thoughts and beliefs by various members. Yet, few groups plunge straight into the Mutuality phase. More often, groups grow into this phase gradually – starting with the Engagement phase.

The equivalent of the Engagement phase within these methods is related to fostering initial trust among members, and that of the Empowerment phase is often considered an unfortunate prerequisite to the period of 'work'. The aim is to shift the group to relatively unstructured yet honest exchanges among the members. Indeed, when further examined, the 'work' stage of facilitative methods may well appear to focus on the dynamics recognised as the Mutuality phase within the inclusive blueprint.

Perhaps it is necessary to stress that all three methods dedicate some time to ending. Within the inclusive blueprint, this period is called 'the Termination phase'. Altogether then, the combinations suggested so far add up to the typology proposed in Figure 6.

Figure 6: Groupwork methods as phases of group development

Engagement Termination Phase	Empowerment phase	Mutuality phase	phase
Directive			Directive
Mediating	Mediating		Mediating
Facilitative		Facilitative	
Facilitative			

Starting from the left column, all methods share the Engagement phase. Moving to the right, Mediating methods emphasise the dynamics of the Empowerment phase. Further to the right, Facilitative methods focus on the dynamics of the Mutuality phase. Yet, all end up sharing the dynamics of the Termination phase at the far right end of the table.

If the various methods of groupwork are different ways of focusing on different stages of group development, then each practitioner can follow a different method while all share the same language. This is the hallmark of inclusive groupwork. Here it is possible only to point out to possible implications for practice.

Implications for practice: Inclusiveness

The inclusive stance is grounded in a systemic framework articulated elsewhere (Manor, 2000a, pp.33-96). One of the practice implications of this stance is that the phases of Engagement and Termination are always needed. Yet, in between these two, various phases and different crises may or may not appear in each group. Only those stages that are needed to pursue members' identified goals have to be included in practice. These stages can be mapped out as different combinations of three major aspects: process, structure and contents. Each of these aspects can then be more concretely described, but for the present purpose these details are not entirely necessary. At a more general level - here are the implications of Figure 6:

- Discrete quality of life goals may be advanced through directive methods. Examples may be goals related to work and education. Directing linear learning, practitioners who follow these methods will remain in a central position and work in a structured way. By doing so, these practitioners will extend the dynamics of the Engagement phase as understood within the inclusive blueprint.
- Composite quality of life goals may be pursued through mediating methods. Examples of such goals are various social relations. In this case, the practitioner will adopt an intermediate position in the group and focus on mediating learning experiences that arise out of interaction among group members. From an inclusive point of view, such a practitioner will extend the Empowerment phase to become the major mode of learning in the group.
- Holistic quality of life goals may be promoted through facilitative methods; addressing goals such as clients' positive self-concept. Such an emphasis will mean that this practitioner will opt for a variable position in the group and focus on

facilitating experiential learning. Such a focus will amount to extending the Mutuality phase of the inclusive blueprint – turning that phase into the main learning experience in the group.

Of course, clients may identify very different goals. It is possible to wish to find a job and, at the same time, want to have more friends. This may just mean that practitioners will have to increase their versatility. In principle, there is no reason why any practitioner will have to remain restricted to one method. Over time, and with added training and experience, each practitioner can expand the range of groupwork methods she uses. Each can add any of the relevant methods and still practise within an internally coherent framework.

The point here is not to prescribe another model – too many are probably available by now. Rather, the point is to ensure that models are used to fit the identified purposes.

Summary and comments: The need for training

How are these ideas related to the role of groupwork in mental health practice? Here are the implications of the discussion in relation to the three aims mentioned at the beginning:

Diversity: addressing different clients' needs

It may be possible to define clients' needs as quality of life goals. One advantage of doing this is that these goals have already been broken down into a researchable range of questions that clients can easily answer. If we see the helping process as a form of learning, then accomplishing each goal is similar to achieving a particular learning outcome.

Seen as learning outcomes, quality of life goals can be looked at afresh: as outcomes of learning; each requiring different learning experiences. Such a view seems to lead us into classifying these goals into three types: discrete, composite and holistic.

When we look at quality of life goals as targets for learning, different means seem to be needed for pursuing these different ends. Discrete goals seem to call for linear learning, composite goals seem to need interactive learning and holistic goals seem to require experiential learning.

At first, such matching of means to ends may appear to be disconnected to current groupwork knowledge. Are we to start building up groupwork knowledge from scratch now? Yet, upon closer examination it is possible to see that well-known groupwork methods may well engender each of these learning experiences. Such an examination suggests that linear learning is often provided by directive approaches. Interactive learning is rather typical of the mediating methods. Experiential learning is very often enabled in facilitative methods of groupwork.

Together, these combinations may well offer a rich pool of interventions that are sufficiently concrete to enable practitioners to meet a great diversity of clearly identifiable clients' needs. Groupwork in mental health may then be directly linked to a vast body of current research into the quality of life and mental health services.

Coherence: finding a unifying framework

The range of quality of life goals is quite wide. If we apply different groupwork methods to each, we may end up with a bewildering assortment of practices. This diversity may be confusing to clients, to workers and to people who are not involved in practice. However, fragmentation is not really necessary.

Each of the groupwork methods can be seen as emphasising a different phase of the same potential sequence of group development. In this paper it was suggested that directive methods are typically offered in ways that resemble the dynamics of the Engagement phase. Mediating methods appear to cultivate the dynamics often seen during the Empowerment phase. Facilitative methods characteristically cherish the dynamics of the Mutuality phase.

It should be added that, within the inclusive stance, all practitioners are expected to form the group appropriately, enable an Engagement phase and take care of the Termination phase.

Beyond that; each can combine different phases to meet the needs of different clients. Furthermore, some groups may then need to go through particular 'crises' – which enable them to transform their dynamics to deal with a new phase.

When a unifying sequence of potential stages connects different forms of interventions, each choice may be more easily understood. This may be so since the sequence of phases that connects the methods is part of the inclusive framework, and that framework is grounded in the systems approach.

Indeed, the systems approach has been adopted by practitioners from many professions. This wide acceptance of the approach probably stems from its versatility. The systems approach; particularly when grounded in general systems theory, can help in a number of ways: accounting for the relationship between parts (members) and whole (the group), addressing the influences between experiences inside and outside the group, and directing attention to adaptation as well as change.

The systems approach has already been applied in many different areas: family therapy, group counselling, organisational development, network analysis and more. By adopting the inclusive stance, groupwork practice can become part of this widely spread view of human relationships. When it does so - groupwork may be more easily understood by other practitioners, by managers and by fund holders.

Systematic evaluation: Finding indicators that can be used by all

We do need to expand the range of groupwork interventions subjected to systematic evaluation. We can begin by logically analysing which groupwork method is likely to generate the learning experiences that lead to the outcomes clients want. If clients want help with work opportunities, we may help them by concentrating on learning how to complete job applications and rehearsing how they may cope in job interviews. Such form of learning may be offered by directive groupwork methods.

If the help clients want is of a different nature; for example, promoting a positive self-concept, then we may logically connect it to other groupwork methods and work with such a group differently – adopting the equally well documented ways of the facilitative methods.

In research terms, this form of logical matching is concerned with establishing the validity of what we do. Indeed, the bulk of this paper was dedicated to exploring the possible validity of various connections among different bodies of well established knowledge.

Next we shall want to know whether our work with each group resulted in what clients wanted it to be. Fortunately, it is by now easier to find the answer. We can do what many in mental health services have done: we can give each client the questionnaire called Lancashire Quality of Life Profile (Oliver et al., 1996, pp.251-264), and ask each to complete it. We shall have to do this three times: before the group begins, when the group ends and at a follow up date. Yet, as this questionnaire has been widely used by now (Oliver 1999) it should not be too difficult to analyse the results meaningfully. The results can be discussed with each client, each care manager and each fund holder. Each can then suggest how to further improve each client's quality of life.

For such groupwork to be fit for purpose, all three conditions – diversity, coherence and systematic evaluation, are necessary.

Finally – is this really going to happen? Not really, unless. Unless groupworkers are consciously trained to see groupwork in these terms. Indeed: the question of groupwork training in mental health inevitably arises out of these pages. In our study mentioned before (Papps et al. 2003) only 36.9% of mental health practitioners said that they had received specialised training in groupwork, while many more - 87.5% of them, said they wanted such training.

Is it so difficult to think of a groupwork course structured to meet mental health needs? Such a course can present students with the rich and well documented heritage of three major groupwork traditions: directive, mediating and facilitative. Indeed, our study (Papps, 2003) suggested that mental health practitioners clustered groupwork methods in a similar fashion. Practitioners tended to associate various cognitive-behavioural methods with one another, and these were included in the directive methods discussed here. These practitioners also tended to group together various methods that have been practised within social group work, and these correspond to the mediating methods explored here. Finally, mental health practitioners also identified a psychotherapeutic range, and this range is included in the facilitative methods identified here.

These three wide sources can then be combined within a systemic view of groupwork; for example, that suggested by the inclusive stance. It will be necessary to combine direct practice with clients groups as forms of supervised fieldwork placements on such a course. Part of that placement could then be to administer the Lancashire Quality of Life Profile (Oliver et al., 1996, pp.251-264) to each client at agreed times. Students will then present accounts of their work and results of their efforts as forms of assessment, not dissimilar to the use of portfolios on other groupwork courses (Doel et al. 2002).

Yes, a great deal of work is still to be done. This paper is a proposal for action research in groupwork as applied to mental health. It is suggested that by adopting an inclusive framework practitioners may expand the range of interventions coherently, relate these systematically to identifiable goals and account for their work in terms that can be incorporated into the Care Programme Approach. I would be delighted to hear from those interested in pursuing such an endeavour.

References

Barlow, D. H. and Durand, V.M. (1995) *Abnormal psychology: An integrative approach.* London: Brooks/Cole

Berg, R. C., Landreth, G.L. and Fall, K.A. (1998) *Group Counselling.* London: Accelerated Development. 3rd edition

Bleach, A. and Ryan, P. (1995) *Community Support for Mental Health.* Brighton: Pavillion

Brooker, C. and Repper, J. (Eds.) (1998) *Serious Mental Health Problems in the Community: Policy, practice and research.* London: Balliere Tindall

Brown, N. (1998) *Psycho-Educational Groups.* London: Accelerated Development

Department of Health (1995) *Building Bridges: A guide to arrangements for inter-city working for the care and protection of severely mentally ill people.* London: HMSO

Department of Health (1999) *Modernising Mental Health Services: Safe, sound and supportive.* London: Department of Health

Department of Health (2000) *Reforming the Mental Health Act.* London: Department of Health

Doel, M. and Sawdon, C. (2000) No group is an island: Groupwork in a social work agency. in O. Manor (Ed.) *Ripples: Groupwork in Different Settings.* London: Whiting and Birch pp.65-84

Doel, M., Sawdon, C. and Morrison, D. (2002) *Learning, Practice and Assessment: Signposting the portfolio.* London: Jessica Kingsley

Durkin, J.E. (1981) *Living Groups: Group psychotherapy and general systems theory.* New York: Brunner/Mazel

Finlay, L. (1993) Groupwork. in J. Creek (Ed.) *Occupational Therapy and Mental Health.* Edinburgh: Churchill Livingston

Finlay, L. (2000) When actions speak louder: Groupwork in occupational therapy. in O. Manor (Ed.) *Ripples: Groupwork in different settings. London:* Whiting and Birch, pp.32-42

Forster, S. (Ed.) (1997) *The A-Z of Community Mental Health Practice.* Cheltenham: Stabley Thorns

Freeman, M., Miller, C., and Ross, N. (2000) The impact of individual philosophies of teamwork on multi-professional practice and the implications for education. *Journal of Interprofessional Care*, 14, 3, 237-247

Gitterman, A. and Shulman, L. (Eds.) (1994) *Mutual Aid Groups: Vulnerable populations and the life cycle.* New York: Columbia University Press. 2nd edition

Hardcastle, D.A., Wencour, S.P. and Powers, P.R. (1997) *Community Practice: Theories and skills for social workers.* Oxford: Oxford University Press

Hartley, P. (1997) *Group Communication.* London: Routledge

Hatzimitriadou, R.E. (2002) Political ideology, helping mechanisms and empowerment of mental health self-help/mutual aid groups. *Community and Applied psychology*, 12, 4, 271-285

Kaplan, K. L. (1988) *Directive Group Therapy: Innovative mental health treatment.* Thorofare, NJ: Slack

Kolb, D.A. (1984) *Experiential Learning.* Englewood Cliffs, NJ: Prentice-Hall

Lacoursiere, R.B. (1980) *The life Cycle of Groups.* New York: Human Science Press

Lin, N. and Peck, K. (1999) Social networks and mental health. in A.V. Horwitz and T.L. Scheid (Eds.) *A Handbook for the Study Of Mental Health: Social contexts, theories and systems.* Cambridge: Cambridge University Press, pp. 241-258

MacKenzie, R. (1997) *Time-Managed Group Psychotherapy.* London: American Psychiatric Press

Manor, O. (1988) The monitoring of co-active learning in social group work: a pilot study. *Social Work with Groups, 11 (1/2), 17-30*

Manor, O. (1990) Engaging students in co-active learning: Empirical markers. *Issues in Social Work Education, 9, 1/2, 1-52*

Manor, O. (1992) Transactional analysis, object relations and the systems approach: Finding the counterparts. *Transactional Analysis Journal, 22, 1, 4-15*

Manor, O. (2000a) *Choosing a Groupwork Approach: An inclusive stance.* London: Jessica Kingsley

Manor, O. (Ed.) (2000b) *Ripples: Groupwork in different settings.* London: Whiting and Birch

Manor, O. (2000c) Help as mutual aid: Groupwork in mental health. in O. Manor (Ed.) *Ripples: Groupwork in different settings.* London: Whiting and Birch. pp.85-104

Morgan, G. (1997) *Images of Organization.* London: Sage. 2nd edition

Mullender, A. and Ward, D. (1991) *Self-Directed Groupwork: Users take action for empowerment.* London: Whiting and Birch

Oliver, J., Huxley, P., Bridges, K. and Mohamad, H. (1996) *Quality of Life and Mental Health Services.* London: Routledge

Oliver, J.P.L. (1999) How to use quality of life measures in individual care. in S. Priebe, J.P.L. Oliver, and W Kaiser (Eds.) *Quality of Life and Mental Health Care.* Petersfield: Wrighton Biomedical. pp. 82-105

Onyett, S. (2003) *Teamwork in Mental Health.* Basingstoke; Palgrave

Papps, B., Manor, O. and Carson, J. (2003) Using groupwork in community mental health: Practitioners' views. *Groupwork, 13, 3, 6-36*

Pearson, P. and Spencer, J. (1995) Pointers to effective teamwork: Exploring primary care. *Journal of Interprofessional Care, 9, 131-138*

Priebe, S., Oliver, J.P.L. and Kaiser, W. (Eds.) (1999) *Quality of Life and Mental Health Care*. Petersfield: Wrighton Biomedical

Scott, M.J. and Stradling, S.G. (1998) *Brief Group Counselling*. Chichester: John Wiley

Secker, J., Pidd, F. Parham, A. and Peck, E. (2000) Mental health in the community: Roles, responsibilities and organisation of primary care and specialist services. *Journal of interprofessional Care*, 14, 1, 49-58

Shulman, L. (1999) *The Skills of Helping Individuals, Families, Groups, and Communities*. Itasca, IL: Peacock. 4th edition

Smith, K.K. and Berg, D.N. (1987) *Paradoxes of Group Life*. San Francisco: Jossey-Bass

Trower, P., Bryant, B. and Argyle, M. (1978) *Social Skills and Mental Health*. London: Methuen

Trotzer, J. P. (1999) *The Counselor and the Group*. London: Accelerated Development

Tsang, N.M. (1990) *Learning Styles and Associated Learning Barriers on a Social Work Course in Hong Kong*. Unpublished PhD dissertation. London: Middlesex University

Wilson, J. (1995) *How to Work with Self-Help Groups*. Aldershot: Ashgate

Yalom, I.D. (1995) *The Theory And Practice Of Group Psychotherapy*. New York: Basic Books. 4th edition

This chapter was first published in 2003 in *Groupwork* Vol. 13(3), pp.101-128

At the time of writing, Oded Manor was Principal Lecturer in Social Work, School of Health and Social Sciences, Middlesex University

Strengths and weaknesses of self-help groups in mental health: The case of Grow

Grow is a self-help movement of ex-mental health patients which is well established in Australia. Participant observation of two groups over six months suggested strengths, difficulties and weaknesses. The strengths concerned intense commitment to mutual aid among members, a great deal of sharing and an unusual form of rotating leadership. The difficulties centred on the unstable sources of finance and the unmanageable caseloads of workers. The weaknesses related to the quasi-religious ideology, which might have inhibited the expression and exploration of negative feelings. Possible ways of improving the work of Grow are suggested.

Key words: *self-help; mutual aid; religious ideology*

Introduction

Self-help groups have been important in the rehabilitation of mental health patients in the community. (Durman, 1976; Levy, 1976; Liberman, 1986; Jacob & Goodman, 1989; Kurtz, Mann & Chambon, 1987; Salem, Seidman & Rappaport, 1988; Lavoie, Borkerman & Gidron, 1955)

Jacob and Goodman (1989) estimated that 3.7% of the adult population in the USA were using self-help groups. Self-help groups were shown to be an effective and economical mode of mental health treatment (Antz, 1976; Hurvita, 1974; Riessman, 1965; Katz, 1970 and Vattano, 1972). However, many self-help groups are not flexible in their practice and are not open to new members. Also, they may help their members to cope rather than to challenge the existing values and service in the society (Henry, 1976). These groups may not be able to cooperate with professionals in dealing with their own problems (Bryant, 1990; Cheslear, 1990). Members in these self-help groups are more concerned with how they feel. They do not look into the social causes of their problems (Dewer, 1976; Lemberg, 1984; Sidel & Sidel, 1976 and Gartner & Riessman, 1977). They may run a risk of collective self-stigmatization and self-labelling (Kingree & Ruback, 1994). Furthermore, Parkinson (1979) pointed out that self-help groups were not subjected to public accountability. They may avoid social change and turn clients into victims of their problems.

In this paper, the writer describes the findings of a study of two self-help groups belonging to Grow in South Australia. There were five research questions in this study:

1. What were the general characteristics of these self-help groups?
2. In what ways did Grow Groups help the Grow Members?
3. What were the strengths of the Grow Group?
4. What were the weaknesses of the Grow Group?
5. How did the Growers perceive these weaknesses?

In this paper, 'self-help group' means a 'voluntary association among many individuals who share a common need or problem and who seek to use the group as a means of dealing with their needs or problems' (Durman, 1976:433). Grow is a self-help group because it is a voluntary association, with ex-mental health patients coming together to use the group as a valid means for social interaction and social rehabilitation.

Research method

Grow in Australia and the Observed Grow Group

Grow is a famous self-help movement for mental health patients in Australia (Toro, Rappoport & Seidman, 1987). The movement began in Sydney in 1975 when a group of former patients borrowed the model from Alcoholics Anonymous. They applied the Twelve Steps of Recovery to the rehabilitation of mental health patients. At first it was known as Recovery Group. Later as more people joined in, they changed the name to Grow. Eventually, Grow had over 400 groups throughout Australia and expanded to other countries (Keogh, 1975: introduction). Each Grow Group was self-supporting through voluntary donations made by members at the weekly meetings. The early financing of Grow was informal, with small and spontaneous offerings from its members. Later, it attracted support from private donors. Subsequently, the Federal and State government offered financial subsidies to Grow. At the time of this study, Grow still relied on a combination of voluntary and official funds in varying proportions in the different states in Australia (Grow, 1981). In South Australia, the State Government funded about 60% of expenditure. The state coordinator and fieldworkers in Grow of South Australia were employed full time. Before they had become full time workers, they had been members; called Growers, for many years.

For the sake of confidentiality, the writer cannot disclose the locations of the two observed groups. Like other Grow Groups, they had three to fifteen members in each group. Both had been established for four to five years by the time of the writer's observation. Group members were either ex-mental health patients or persons with mental health problems. Informed consents were obtained from them to conduct this study.

Data collection

Participant observation (Jorgensen, 1989) was used in the study because Grow was a voluntary, self-help, and anonymous project. It did not keep any case records or personal information on its members. Also, the group process and dynamics of those self-help groups were unknown to outsiders. Thus, it seemed better to experience and observe the groups through informal social interaction, direct observation and formal interviews (McCall & Simmon, 1969:1). The researcher used a 'dual entry' (Schatzman, 1964) to the groups. He gained permission both from the coordinator of the Grow in South Australia and group members before starting the observation. In addition, two groups were observed to ensure that what the researcher observed was not the unique characteristics of a particular Grow Group. Over about six months, the researcher had frequent informal social interaction by way of having lunch and making telephone contact with group members. Also, he participated in every weekly meeting of these two groups. He conducted formal interviews with three field workers and the service coordinator. Furthermore, he collected newsletters, annual reports and training materials produced by Grow in Australia. During every group meeting, he took brief notes about the group process. To ensure credibility, fieldworkers in these two groups read and commented on those notes. Gold (1958) described four possible roles of the researcher in participant observation. These are: complete participant, participant-as-observer, observer-as-participant, and complete observer (Gold, 1958:217). In the first month, as a complete observer, the researcher observed two groups without making comment. In the next two months, entering the role of observer-as participant, the researcher shared his feelings or opinions. For the following three months, as a participant-as-observer, the researcher participated in the group process like other members. To avoid 'going native' to the point of losing his objectivity, the researcher avoided the role of a complete participant. He withdrew from casual social gatherings, informal home visits and recreational activities among members in these two groups.

Data analysis and triangulation

Grounded Theory guided the analysis of the data. This type of analysis has four stages: comparing the data applicable to each conceptual category; integrating the categories and their properties; delimiting the emergent theory, and writing up the theory (Glazer and Strauss, 1967, pp.105-115). In running through the various sources of data, the writer formulated categories that were relevant to the research questions. Then, the relationships between these categories were examined. Finally, the writer tried to formulate concepts about the strengths and weaknesses of the Grow Groups. In order to triangulate the findings, the researcher shared his findings with the state coordinator of the Grow in South Australia. The coordinator was a well-trained and experienced social worker. Also, the findings were shared with some experienced members in these two groups. Their comments and suggestions were incorporated in the process of data analysis and presentation.

Findings

Characteristics of the groups

The general characteristics of group members in these two groups are described in Tables 1 and 2 below. Their personal identities have been properly disguised to ensure confidentiality.

Principles underlying practice

To evaluate the experiences involved one has to know something about the ideas and practices that characterised these groups. However, only brief comments can be offered here.

The Structured Philosophy

After many years of experience, Growers developed their own philosophy, insights and group methods. In Grow, every group member is considered to be inadequate or maladjusted. Maladjustment and inadequacy is a process of decline (Grow, 1982:3), and the process of decline has twelve steps. The declining person moves from being egocentric, to becoming totally self-absorbed and finally to being fixated in psychotic delusion and hallucination. Maturity is needed to counter such a deteriorating process. The key in striving for maturity is to get well. In the process of maturity, one should get rid of the excess interest in oneself and find out about others' interests (Keogh, 1981, p.5) There are 12 steps to achieving maturity which is a process of softening defence, rebuilding the inner self and establishing ways to contact the outer-world.

Growers have their own insights into dealing with various types of maladjustments and inadequacies. These insights are compiled in three books that contain the 'Grow Wisdom'. The Growers call these the Blue, the Red, and the Brown Books (Grow, 1982; Keogh, 1975 & 1981). Grow Wisdom is the source of support and insights into problem solving for every member.

The structured group method

A prescribed 'Group Method' instructs the Growers what to share and how to share in great detail. Each group session lasts for about two hours and is divided into five sections, as follows:

> 5 minutes for 'Opening Routine', 30-35 minutes for ' Group Interaction',
> 20-30 minutes for 'Middle Routine', 25-30 minutes for 'Resumed
> Interaction' and 15 minutes for 'Closing Routine'. (Grow, 1983)

In the Opening, Middle and Closing Routines, Growers are
required to recite together certain messages from the Blue Book
to ensure their commitment to one another and mutual trust.
During the periods of Group Interaction and Resumed Interaction,
Growers share their own feelings, problems and insights. Drawing
on suggestions and interpretations from Grow Wisdom, they help
one another to resolve their personal problems.

Strengths of the structured approach

The Twelve Steps Miracle

The structured group method of Grow originated from the famous
Twelve Steps of Recovery developed by Alcoholics Anonymous.
Dupont (1997) described this experience as a 'Modern Miracle'
in which effective techniques help people conquer destructive
behaviours and rebuild their self worth and a healthy lifestyle. In
the same way, the twelve steps programme in Grow can remove
the group members' self-defeating denial of mental illness. The
framework offers Growers practical ways to deal with their life
difficulties. It helps them achieve successful health and realistic
self worth in the process of their rehabilitation.

Mutual sharing and rotating leadership

Mutual cooperation was stressed in every group session of
both groups. It was assumed that every group member had the
responsibility to share, to accept, to respect and to support one
another in the process that led to maturity (Grow, 1982:72-9). A
hierarchy of membership existed. A Newcomer was accepted as an
observer of the Grow Group. After three meetings, s/he became
a Prospective Grower. After participating for three months, a

Table 1

General characteristics and background of the Observed Group A

1) Committed Grower and Organizer (OA). 6 years
2) Married; stable married life
3) Had been hospitalized; fully recovered for five years
4) Nil
5) Supportive; intellectual; introvert

1) Committed Grower and Leader (LA). 2 years
2) Married; Spouse severely ill; 2 sons (problem youth)
3) Breakdown once; runaway from home; fully recovered for many years
4) Burden of spouse's illness; heavy parental roles
5) Social; helpful

1) Committed Grower (1A). 3 years
2) Divorced; 3 daughters
3) Attempted suicide; self pity; loneliness; depressed
4) Accommodation problem; loneliness
5) Social; defensive

1) Committed Grower (2A). $1^1/_2$ years
2) Single; Brother is also schizophrenic; Single parent
3) Psychotic relapse twice; outpatient in a clinic
4) Psychotic disturbances; active hallucinations
5) Introvert

1) Prospective Grower (3A). 3 to 4 times
2) Single
3) Bipolar disorder; Recently discharged from hospital; still unstable
4) Loss of control of temperament in manic episode
5) Impulsive

1) Newcomer (4A) twice
2) Married; unhappy marital relationship; extra-marital sex
3) Breakdown once; now fairly stable; strong guilt feeling
4) Trying to retain their marriage
5) Sophisticated

1) Newcomer (5A) twice
2) Married; pressure from parents
3) Breakdown once; fairly stable
4) Trying to escape from parental influence
5) Verbal; social

Key to table 1 and 2
(1) Status and experience in the group. (2) Family background.
(3) Mental health history. (4) Presenting problem.
(5) Attitudes and performance in the group.

Table 2
General Characteristics and Background of the Observed Group B

(1) Committed Grower and Organizer (OB1) 7 years
(2) Being an orphan in childhood; divorced and single
(3) Breakdown four times and medical defaulter for five years; later joined Grow, received treatment and fully recovered for six years
(4) Nil
(5) Kind-hearted and helpful

(1) Committed Grower and Organizer (OB2) 6 years
(2) Married, unhappy marital life
(3) Breakdown and late recovered; depressive mode
(4) Martial discord, sense of guilt
(5) Emotionally unstable and self-blaming

(1) Committed Grower and Leader (LB) 2 years
(2) Single and living with sibling
(3) Paranoia and later recovered; some obsessive delusions of having sex with his/her sibling
(4) Annoyed by his or her obsessive thoughts
(5) Pleasant and nice but a bit suspicious with others

(1) Committed Grower and Recorder (RB1) 1 year
(2) Stable family with two daughters
(3) Suicidal attempt with depressive moods but under control by medication
(4) Child rearing problems
(5) Helpful but introvert

(1) Committed Grower and Recorder (RB2) 6 months
(2) Stable family with parents, but parents were controlling
(3) Schizophrenic patient in outpatient clinic
(4) Relationship problems with parents
(5) Nervous

(1) Prospective Grower (4B) 2 months
(2) Single
(3) Bipolar disorder, on medication
(4) Control of temperament
(5) Impulsive

(1) Prospective Grower (5B) 5 times
(2) Single parent with three children
(3) Affective psychosis recently discharged from hospitals
(4) Child rearing problems
(5) Helpful

Prospective Grower became a Committed Grower. If nominated by group members, s/he became the Organizer of the Group. Leadership changed every session among Committed Growers. If there were insufficient numbers of Committed Growers in the group, the leading role fell to the Prospective Growers. Yet, sometimes hierarchical divisions were ignored. For example, in Group A, members (2A), (3A), (4A), and (5A) were either Newcomers or seen as unstable. Moreover, (1A) was seen as a bit defensive during the period of group sharing. Therefore, (LA) took up the leading role during most group sessions. When (LA) was absent, (OA) would take up the leading role. In Group B, (RB1), (RB2) and (LB) were seen as stable and experienced Committed Growers. Indeed, they took turns in assuming the leading role.

Good connections with external parties

Grow is widely recognized in Australia. During the time of this study, the Prime Minister of South Australia and the South Australian Health Commissioner were the patrons. Furthermore, Grow was partly financed by the State Government. Grow had good connections with professionals and many of them; social workers, psychologists, psychiatrists and mental health workers recommended Grow to their clients. Grow was also well received in the community. Many newcomers came to Grow because of an introduction by their friends or their neighbours, who had heard about the good work of Grow. Finally, some fieldworkers in Grow were trained social workers. Before they were employed as full time workers, they had been Committed Growers for many years. They promoted good communication between social work practice and the organisation of Grow.

Perceived difficulties

The following difficulties in running the Grow Group were mentioned by Growers.

Irregular Funding

As Grow was partly funded by the State and partly by private donation, funding is rather irregular. Payments varied from time to time or from group to group. For example, Group A was better funded than Group B because one member's relative donated a large sum of money. Group A seemed to organize more outdoor activities, more snacks in tea breaks and better programme materials than those in Group B. The fieldworkers frankly admitted that irregular funding sometimes even affected their salaries and continuity of employment.

Insufficient Manpower and Resources

Insufficient manpower was always a problem in maintaining the Grow Group. All Growers were voluntary. Only fieldworkers and the state coordinator were full time workers employed by the Grow. The time and effort that individual Growers contributed to the work varied too. For instance, because of personal problems, the organizer of Group A (OA), was unable to take up the leading role for a month. In Grow, each fieldworker had to look after more than ten Grow Groups. Fieldworkers in Group A and Group B complained that they did not have time to look after those members with personal difficulties, or those who withdrew from the group.

Voluntary Nature and Anonymity

Participation in a Grow Group was purely voluntary and anonymous. On the one hand, it could protect the privacy and confidentiality of individual members and strengthen the self-help nature of the group. On the other hand, the voluntary nature and anonymity could create difficulties in the management and personal care of those Growers in need. The organisation did not keep any personal record of individual members. Because of this, the change of fieldworkers, organisers and group leaders could mean a loss of information and contact with those members who did not appear in the group sessions.

Rehabilitation of chronic mental health patients

Rehabilitation of chronic mental health patients demands resources and community support. Residual symptoms and prolonged institutionalization (Goffman, 1961; Barton, 1959; Wing & Brown, 1970) make patients become submissive, withdrawn, passive and inert in interpersonal interaction (Yip, 1992). Most members in these two observed groups were chronic ex-mental health patients. They demanded extra care during episodes of psychiatric relapse. Indeed, Growers supported one another closely in facing personal difficulties and psychiatric relapse. All these were voluntary contributions made by committed Growers. Yet as they were recovered mental health patients, prolonged and over-demanding care of others might even jeopardize their own mental health.

Perceived weaknesses of the structured approach

Weaknesses did not necessary imply a failure of the Grow Group and Grow Programme. Rather, these could be the consequences of the above mentioned difficulties. The fieldworkers and the state coordinator in Grow were in agreement concerning the validity of the following weaknesses identified.

Non-evaluativeness and subjectivity

In the two observed groups, Growers had to fill in the Weekly Evaluation Sheet. Organizers and Recorders had to fill in the Bi-monthly Evaluation Sheet. Yet these forms of evaluation were rather limited. Firstly, the evaluation sheets were actually designed within the terms of the Grow Wisdom, rather than from any other perspectives and so they did not provide information that was comparable to outcomes elsewhere. Secondly, Grow was anonymous by nature. It did not keep any case history and personal record of members. This could inhibit formal assessment and evaluation; in particular, long-term case study of the effect of the Grow Group. Furthermore, most of the Grow Wisdom, Programme and Group Methods were derived from subjective collective experience of previous Growers. These might have been effective in most situations, but might have neglected certain areas of rehabilitation. In addition, Growers were encouraged to testify only about the successful effects and not the failure of the Grow Method. In two observed groups, the researcher noted that whenever any group members challenged the Grow Wisdom, Committed Growers tended to respond in one or more of the following ways:

- Encourage the member to clarify whether it was individual problems or the problem of Grow Wisdom.
- State that the member was not familiar with the Grow Wisdom.
- Recite the books of Grow and let the member read some passage to make sure that Grow Wisdom was not wrongly interpreted.
- Say that the opinions would be noted down and should be considered in the Organizers and Recorders Meetings.

The Quasi-Religious Cults

The twelve steps miracle described before, could be interpreted as a healthy lifestyle (Dunpont, 1997) but also as a form of quasi-religious ideology about mental health and mental illness. In particular, the Grow Commitment - recited by every Grower in the Opening, Middle and Closing Routine - might be interpreted as quasi-religious ritual. Similarly, the unchallenged Grow Wisdom might become the Grow 'Bible'. The writer asked the Growers how they felt about these rituals and ceremonies. Some said they really enjoyed them. Some newcomers said they could not really feel the warmth and empathy behind the 'ceremony'. One even said that she felt under pressure to follow the discussion guidelines in the Grow Wisdom and Grow Method. In reality, the ceremony of embracing one another might be common in western culture but it might be embarrassing for Asians. The writer had discussed the moral implications of these quasi-religious cults with the state coordinator and the fieldworkers. They had the following responses:

- All these quasi-religious rituals were not unique to Grow. Instead they were common among self-help groups which followed the twelve steps structured approach of Alcoholics Anonymous.

- The organizers and Committed Growers in every group were fully aware that if anyone did not want to follow the Group Routine or Rituals, they would not force them. They would kindly let this individual observe or participate in any way s/he felt easy. They understood the group pressure faced by the one who did not share the quasi-religious culture. As participation in Grow was entirely voluntary, they would not force anyone to participate or follow the Grow Wisdom and Grow Group. Instead, they would try to explain the meanings and history behind all these rituals. According to their experiences, once the newcomers and Prospective Growers felt the warmth, empathy and support of the Growers, they would gradually enjoy all these rituals.
- They understood the diversity of culture within a multicultural country. Thus, Grow encouraged different ethnic groups to run or design their own Grow Groups. Right now, they were formulating some groups for the Asians. They offered some Chinese translation of the Grow Wisdom for the writer's comment.

Regarding their responses, the writer wondered whether Chinese culture might have different ways of interpreting mental illness and recovery. Therefore it might not be appropriate to adopt a straight translation of the Grow Wisdom. Instead, the Chinese Grow Group might have to formulate its own wisdom in dealing with mental illness.

Uncontrollable Workload for the Worker

In Grow, the full time fieldworker and state coordinators were former experienced Committed Growers. To avoid dominating the Groups, they tried to adopt an indirect supervisory role by identifying themselves as ordinary Growers only. By retaining this identity, they could participate in informal visits and gatherings with other Growers naturally. However, that identity might also lead to uncontrollable workload and confusing client-worker relationships. Sometimes, workers invited other Growers to their homes for dinner. They were ready to answer telephone calls from any member in the group at any times, especially in crises. That meant that they had to work overtime and even during their private hours. As a result they might easily burn-out. One of the fieldworkers told the writer that she did not have a private life. Even her family members, especially her husband were involved in helping other Growers.

Inhibiting the expression of feelings

Grow emphasizes objective thinking. Growers are required to be conscious about their thinking and feelings. In their Blue Book, ways to control feelings are explained. First, there are the 'Six Rules for Objective Thinking'. Then there is the 'Rational Way to Express Feeling'. Finally, there is the 'Way to Evaluate Feelings'. These mean that feelings have to be disciplined through rational thinking. In both groups, the writer observed incidents when members who expressed intense negative feelings; such as anger, aggression or sadness, were disciplined by organizers and Committed Growers. Similar findings were identified by Toro, Rappaport, and Seidman (1987). They carried out a Group Social Climate comparison between 33 mutual help groups from Grow International and 25 psychotherapy groups. The results showed that members in the Grow Group saw their groups as higher in regard to cohesion, leader support, independence, task orientation, order and organization and leader control, but lower in relation to expressiveness, anger and aggression, and innovation (Toro, Rappaport and Seidman, 1987). The highly structured Group Routines that were part of the Grow Wisdom, seemed to inhibit the direct ventilation of complicated feelings such as anger, frustration, and aggression. In Grow, personal victorious testimonies of success by individual Growers were highly stressed as vivid examples of the achievements of Grow Wisdom. For example, the writer noted that after a 'beautiful' and 'constructive' victorious personal testimony offered by a Grower, it was very hard for other Growers to express their negative feelings towards themselves or others.

Dropout of newcomers

Participation in Grow is strictly voluntary (Grow, 1981: 3). Growers can come and go as they wish. It is believed that only those who want Grow and trust it may benefit from it. For example, in Group A, there were two newcomers who attended only one session. In Group B, there were several newcomers who withdrew after one or two sessions. Some Growers returned to the group after one or two years of being away. It seemed that the follow up of newcomers was inadequate. Apart from some briefing and telephone contact after the first group session, there was no further follow up actions in the two observed Grow Groups. Indeed, the sharing circle of Committed Growers with its quasi-religious cult might have been too closed for the newcomers to break into it. Newcomers might be frightened by the very frank sharing of information among group members about their private lives. As a result, they might keep quiet and withdraw from such intense sharing. Many Committed Growers in these two groups frankly admitted that they spent from half to one year tuning into the sharing and caring community of Grow.

Suggested improvements

Faced by the above weaknesses, Growers in the observed groups had different attitudes:

- They were unaware of these weaknesses (mainly Newcomers and some Prospective Growers).
- They thought that they were the characteristics of the Grow Group (mostly Committed Growers).
- They were aware of these weaknesses but thought that there was no way to change them, and there was no better model (most Committed Growers)
- They were aware of these weaknesses and tried to improve them but failed (one Organizer and fieldworkers).
- They were aware of these weaknesses and tested ways of overcoming them (fieldworkers, one Organizer and the State Coordinator)

In regard to the last view, Organizers, fieldworkers and the State Coordinator had run some orientation groups within the mental hospitals in an attempt to introduce and prepare mental health patients to joining Grow Groups upon their discharge. Furthermore, they had cooperated with some academic researchers and had done research to evaluate the Grow Model. However, most Growers were not aware of these weaknesses and they were psychologically and socially dependent on the Grow model. Therefore, any drastic change and severe criticisms seemed to be inappropriate. Bearing in mind the limitations of this study the writer would like to suggest the following areas for further exploration.

Further research and evaluation

Grow may consider further study in the following areas:

- The psychosocial and medical needs of the Growers.
- The effects of internalising the Grow Wisdom on the Growers.
- The therapeutic effects of the Grow Group on the Growers.
- The formal and informal mutual support system among Growers.
- Integration of the Grow Model with the larger community.

Longitudinal case studies may be carried out in these areas to show that the Grow Model is effective in rehabilitating mental health patients.

Diversity of interpretation of the Grow Wisdom and Method

Diversity in running Grow Groups and interpreting the Grow Wisdom may be allowed. Individual groups may be allowed to have their own ways of following the Scheduled Group Method. Sometimes, group members may need more in-depth sharing of feeling. Sometimes, the group may want to discuss the implementation of tasks and activities. Also, personal testimonies of failure may be encouraged as these can shed further light on personal problems and complicated feelings experienced by the group members. Various ethnic groups may be encouraged to formulate their own wisdom in dealing with life stresses and painful experiences. The same may be applied to Growers with different class structures, geographical origins, occupations, age groups and family backgrounds.

Orientation to newcomers

Introductory Grow Groups for newcomers may to be established so that they become used to the particular ways of sharing of inner self and the Grow Programme. Follow up of those who drop out may help to make sure that people who failed to join receive sufficient support outside the Grow Group and also find out why they dropped out. These people may have some critical comments about the Grow Model, or they may wish to adjust to the sharing pattern of Growers in the Grow Group. The former can be helpful for reflection and the evaluation of the existing Grow Model.

Community integration and recovery

In some respects, the Grow model appears to be rather similar to the Clubhouse model in psychiatric rehabilitation (Bear, Propst and Malamud, 1982). In both cases the Grow Group clients with mental problems use their own wisdom and their own strengths to resolve their own problems and the organization is run by the clients themselves. However, the Grow Group crystallizes certain strengths in the form of Twelve Steps peer-psychotherapy, and structured group methods that aim to promote a certain understanding of maturity. The Clubhouse model transforms the self-help spirit into a search for vocational rehabilitation and integration into the community through the concepts of 'recovery' and 'rehabilitation' (Deegan, 1996; Bridges, Huxley & Oliver, 1994). The Grow Model can be enriched by the ideas from the Clubhouse model. For example, the Grow Group may include more discussion about helping members to search for open employment. In particular, step 10 of the Twelve Steps of Personal Growth, ('We took our responsible and caring place in our society') may include topics such as searching for open employment, advocating the rights of mental health patients and educating the community against stigmatization and discrimination of mental illness (Fisher & Sartorius, 1999). Based on the writer's several months of participant observation, this paper is an account of the existing strengths, difficulties and weaknesses of the Grow Model in South Australia. In no way does the writer depreciate the contribution of the Grow Model for psychiatric rehabilitation. Grow is still one of the strongest self-help projects for ex-mental health patients in Australia. It is client centred and has developed its own organizational structure. The movement is highly appreciated by both medical and social work professionals in the fields of psychiatric rehabilitation. Nevertheless, more awareness of its weaknesses may stimulate further improvement of its effectiveness and its contribution to the rehabilitation of clients with mental health problems.

References

Antze, P. (1976) The role of ideologies in peer psychotherapy: three case studies. *Journal of Applied Behavioural Science*, 12, 323-345

Barton, R. (1959) *Institutional Neurosis*. Bristol: John Wright

Beard, J., Propst, R. and Malamud, T. (1982) The Fountain house model in psychiatric rehabilitation. *Psychosocial Rehabilitation*, 5, 47-53

Black, R.B. and Drachman, D. (1985) Hospital social workers and self-help groups. *Health and Social Work*, 10,2, 95-103

Bridges, P., Huxley, P. and Oliver, J. (1994) Psychiatric rehabilitation redefined for the 1990s. *The International Journal of Social Psychiatry*, 40, 1-16

Bryant, N. (1990) Self-help groups and professionals: Cooperation or conflict. in A. Katz & E, Bender (Eds.) *Helping One Another: Self-help groups in a changing world.* Oakland: Third Party Publishing

Cheslear, M.A. (1990) The dangers of self-help groups: Understanding and challenging professionals. in T.J. Powell (Ed.) *Working with Self-help Groups.* New York: NASW Press

Deegan, P. (1996) Recovery as a journey of the heart. *Psychiatric Rehabilitation Journal*, 19, 3, 91-97

Dewer, T. (1976) *Self-help and Health: A Report.* New York: City University of New York

Dunpont, R.L. (1997) *The Selfish Brain: Learning from addiction*. New York: American Psychiatric Association

Durman, E.C. (1976) The role of self-help groups in human service. *Journal of Behavioural Science*. 12, 433-440

Fisher, W. and Sartorius N. (1999) (Ed.) *The Image of Madness*. Basel: Karger

Gartner, A. and Riessman, F. (1977) *Self-help in Human Service*. London: Jossey Boss

Glazer, B.C. and Strauss A.L. (1967) *The Discovery of Grounded Theory*. Chicago: Aline

Goffman, E. (1961) *Asylum*. New York: Doubleday

Gold, R.L. (1958) Roles in sociological field observation. *Social Forces*, 36, 217-233

Grow (1976) *Grow, Personal Stories and Testimonies*. Sydney: Grow Publication

Grow (1981) *Grow, Organizers' Training Manual*. Sydney: Grow Publication

Grow (1982) *Grow, the Program of Growth to Maturity*. Sydney: Grow Publication

Grow (1983) *Grow, the Group Method*. Sydney: Grow Publication

Grow Bimonthly Newsletter (S.A. Branch) (1983) Nov-Dec, Sydney: Grow Publication

Henry, S. (1976) The dangers of self-help group. *New Society*, 22, 654-6.

Hurvitz, N. (1974) Peer self-help psychotherapy groups: Psychotherapy without psychotherapists. in R.B Trice (Ed.) *The Sociology of Psychotherapy*. New York: Aronson

Jacobs, M.K. and Goodman, G. (1989) Psychology and self-help groups, predictions on partnership, *American Psychologist*, 44, 536-545

Jorgensen D.L. (1989) *Participant Observation: A methodology for human studies*. London: Sage

Katz, A.H. (1970) Self organization and volunteer participation in social welfare. *Social Work*, 20, 51-60

Keogh, C.B. (1975) (Ed.) *Readings for Mental Health*. Sydney: Grow Publication

Keogh, C.B. (1981) (Ed.) *Readings for Recovery*. Sydney: Grow Publication

Kingree, J.B. and Ruback, R.B. (1994) Understanding self-help groups. in T.J. Powell (Ed.) *Understanding the Self-help Organization*. London: Sage, pp.272-292

Kurtz, L.F. (1990) The self-help movement: Review of the past decade of research. *Social Work with Groups*, 13, 1, 101-115

Kurtz, L.F., Mann, K.B. and Chambon, A. (1987) Linking between social workers and mental health mutual aid groups. *Social Work in Health Care*, 13, 69-78

Lavoie, F., Borkerman, T., and Gidron, B. (1995) *Self-help and Mutual Aid Groups: International and multicultural perspectives*. Binghamton, NY: Haworth

Lemberg B. (1984) Ten ways of self-help groups to fail. *Journal of Orthopsychiatry*, 43, 648-650

Levy L. (1976) Self-help groups: Types and psychological process. *Journal of Applied Behavioural Science*, 12, 311-321

Liberman, M. (1986) Self-help groups and psychiatry. *American Psychiatric Association: Annual Review*, 5, 744-760

McCall, G.J. and Simmons J.L. (1969) *Issues in Participant Observation*. Sydney: Wesley

Parkinson, C. (1979) *The Self-help Movement in Australia*. Australian Council of Social Service

Riessman, F. (1965) The helper therapy principle. *Social Work*, 10, 1, 27-32

Salem, D.A., Seidman, E. and Rappaport, J. (1988) Community treatment of the mentally ill: The promise of mutual-help organization. *Social Work*, 19, 3, 403-408

Sidel, V.W. and Sidel, R. (1976) Beyond coping. Social Policy, 7(1), 67-69

Schatzman, L. (1964) The process of fieldwork. in A. Strauss (Ed.) *Psychiatric Ideologies and Institutions*. New York: Free Press

Toro, P.A., Rappaport, J. and Seidman, E. (1987) Social climate comparison of mutual help and psychotherapy groups. *Journal of Consulting and Clinical Psychology*, 55, 430-441

Vattano, A.J. (1972) Power to the people: Self-help group. *Social Work*, 3, 1, 7-15

Wing, J. K. and Brown, G. (1970) *Institutionalism and Schizophrenia*. Cambridge: Cambridge University Press

Yip, K.S. (1992) Is life model a practical model in working with the mentally ill? A discussion. *Asia Pacific Journal in Social Work*, 2, 1, 18-26.

This chapter was first published in 2002 in *Groupwork* Vol. 13(2), pp.93-113

At the time of writing, Kam-shing Yip was Associate Professor., Department of Applied Social Studies, Hong Kong Polytechnic University

Lightning Source UK Ltd.
Milton Keynes UK
11 September 2010

159720UK00001B/157/P